T0311401

BUSINESS ANTHROPOLOGY

THE BASICS

Business Anthropology: The Basics is an accessible and engaging introductory text organized around key issues in the field. It introduces readers to the application of anthropological theory and practice to real world examples in industry and will assist students in developing awareness, skill, and perspectives to help address real life situations they encounter in the world.

Topics covered include:

- Defining applied, design and digital anthropology
- Explaining key research methods and approaches used in industry, government, and non-profit sectors
- Investigating issues internal to an organization that assist in managing change
- Covering topics like marketing communications, user experience, product development and entrepreneurship
- Explaining ways for organizations to partner and interact with communities, economics and politics to implement change
- Discussing approaches to encourage public conversation about social issues

Business Anthropology: The Basics is an essential read for students and faculty approaching the subject for the first time.

Timothy de Waal Malefyt is Clinical Professor of Marketing at the Gabelli School of Business, Fordham University, New York. A trained anthropologist with over 15 years of corporate experience in advertising firms, he teaches consumer insights and business anthropology to help students understand issues and solve problems.

The Basics

The Basics is a highly successful series of accessible guidebooks which provide an overview of the fundamental principles of a subject area in a jargon-free and undaunting format.

Intended for students approaching a subject for the first time, the books both introduce the essentials of a subject and provide an ideal springboard for further study. With over 50 titles spanning subjects from artificial intelligence (AI) to women's studies, *The Basics* are an ideal starting point for students seeking to understand a subject area.

Each text comes with recommendations for further study and gradually introduces the complexities and nuances within a subject.

ELT
MICHAEL MCCARTHY AND STEVE WALSH

SOLUTION-FOCUSED THERAPY
YVONNE DOLAN

ACTING (THIRD EDITION)
BELLA MERLIN

BUSINESS ANTHROPOLOGY
TIMOTHY DE WAAL MALEFYT

EATING DISORDERS
ELIZABETH MCNAUGHT, JANET TREASURE, AND JESS GRIFFITHS

TRUTH
JC BEALL AND BEN MIDDLETON

PERCEPTION
BENCE NANAY

C.G.JUNG'S COLLECTED WORKS
ANN YEOMAN AND KEVIN LU

Information Classification: General For a full list of titles in this series, please visit www.routledge.com/The-Basics/book-series/B

BUSINESS ANTHROPOLOGY

THE BASICS

Timothy de Waal Malefyt

NEW YORK AND LONDON

Designed cover image: © Getty Images

First published 2024
by Routledge
605 Third Avenue, New York, NY 10158

and by Routledge
4 Park Square, Milton Park, Abingdon, Oxon OX14 4RN

Routledge is an imprint of the Taylor & Francis Group, an informa business

© 2024 Timothy de Waal Malefyt

The right of Timothy de Waal Malefyt to be identified as author of this work has been asserted in accordance with sections 77 and 78 of the Copyright, Designs and Patents Act 1988.

Library of Congress Cataloging-in-Publication Data
Names: Malefyt, Timothy de Waal, author.
Title: Business anthropology : the basics / Timothy de Waal Malefyt.
Description: New York : Routledge, 2024. | Includes bibliographical references and index.
Identifiers: LCCN 2023032661 (print) | LCCN 2023032662 (ebook) |
ISBN 9781032416090 (hbk) | ISBN 9781032416083 (pbk) |
ISBN 9781003358930 (ebk)
Subjects: LCSH: Business anthropology.
Classification: LCC GN450.8 .M35 2024 (print) | LCC GN450.8 (ebook) |
DDC 338.5--dc23/eng/20231019
LC record available at https://lccn.loc.gov/2023032661
LC ebook record available at https://lccn.loc.gov/2023032662

ISBN: 978-1-032-41609-0 (hbk)
ISBN: 978-1-032-41608-3 (pbk)
ISBN: 978-1-003-35893-0 (ebk)

DOI: 10.4324/9781003358930

Typeset in Bembo
by Taylor & Francis Books

CONTENTS

ACKNOWLEDGEMENTS

This book is not a one-off idea, written as a side project, but reflects my deep involvement and passion over many years of integrating anthropology with business. I first worked in a consumer marketing consultancy (Holen North America) as a fledgling anthropologist in the early 1990s. I thank John Lowe, Rita Denny, Vic Russell, Maryann McCabe and Steve Barnett for this opportunity. Then, after gaining my doctorate degree in 1997, I turned again to industry, this time to work directly in advertising agencies, at AFG, D'Arcy Masius Benton and Bowles, and BBDO. I thank Stu Grau, Mike Bentley, and Martin Straw for the lessons learned and the trust I earned working on many projects and campaigns in advertising. In 2012, a pivot to academia landed me at Fordham's Gabelli School of Business, and has brought me a new wave of lessons, engaging with business faculty and especially my students – all of whom I graciously thank. Teaching what I had practiced over the years has been extremely rewarding and fulfilling.

Thanks also to Routledge (Taylor & Francis) and to a keen editor, Meagan Simpson, for reaching out with the book idea, to Gennifer Eccles for help in assembling the final manuscript, and to Yvonne Doney for thoughtful final edits.

I call out special thanks and gratitude to Robert J. Morais, Elizabeth Briody and Matt Artz for their helpful comments on reviewing book chapters (any mistakes are my own). Thanks also to Gillian Tett, for graciously hosting backyard barbeques and dinners at her NYC home—a memorable site for great conversations among colleagues.

In dedications, though, I have two call outs. Maryann McCabe was my muse from whom I first learned to apply anthropology to a range of business situations. And, Brian Moeran was my muse from whom I learned to take business situations and write about them thoughtfully for scholarly publications. I dedicate this book to both of my muses!

ABOUT THE AUTHOR

Timothy de Waal Malefyt (PhD Anthropology, Brown) is Clinical Professor of Marketing at Gabelli School of Business, Fordham University. Previously, he held executive positions as VP, Director of Consumer Insights at BBDO and D'Arcy advertising agencies, where he led teams to explore cultural approaches to consumer research for developing brand and strategic insights. Tim was conference co-organizer for the Ethnographic Praxis in Industry Conference (EPIC 2014) and has hosted the Business Anthropology Summit (2019) and AAA Career Readiness Commission Conference (2022) at Gabelli. His five books include *Advertising Cultures* (2003); *Advertising and Anthropology* (2012); *Ethics in the Anthropology of Business* (2017); *Magical Capitalism* (2018); and *Women, Consumption and Paradox* (2020), as well as numerous other publications. A Fulbright award grantee, he enjoys frequent presentations at conferences, and serves on a number of editorial boards.

INTRODUCTION TO BUSINESS ANTHROPOLOGY

Business anthropology offers a fresh and urgent way for businesses to operate, create and design new products and services. While it stems from mainstream academic anthropology, it promises exciting new directions for students and practitioners seeking a career in one or more of the fields of technology, finance and banking, healthcare services and medicine, user experience, design and product development, data science, marketing and advertising, corporate business, workplace culture and organizational change, law, and engineering, among other fields. Most importantly, it uses anthropological theories and methods to identify and solve real business and social challenges. Work in business anthropology broadly spans non-profit and for-profit companies, start-ups, entrepreneurial work and government agencies.

Just as many definitions define "anthropology," likewise, many terms define business anthropology. Ann Jordan (2019) informs us that the term "business anthropology" was first applied in the 1980s to refer to anthropologists who studied business as academics, or were based in business and worked in, or for, business. While the field dates to the 1920s and 1930s, the term "business anthropology" did not appear in general usage until the 1990s. Earlier names included "industrial anthropology," which reflected the importance of industry during the years of its popularity in the 1920s through the 1950s; "enterprise anthropology" is a name commonly used in Asia; "anthropology of work" is an anthropological field that predates business anthropology but overlaps in subject matter; "economic anthropology" is another older field with overlapping subject matter; and "applied/practicing anthropology"

DOI: 10.4324/9781003358930-1

are two fields with their own differences, which are used inter-changeably since business anthropology is considered a part. Since business enterprises have increasingly become integrated on a global scale and have extended their reach across humanity in virtually every community around the world, now is a crucial time for anthropologists to be actively engaged in influencing such enterprises.

As provost at King's College Cambridge, Gillian Tett (who is also an anthropologist) writes in her book, *Anthro-Vision* (2021), that anthropology can better equip companies to see laterally and recognize issues they might not typically consider. She advocates that anthropology provides an intellectual framework that "enables you to see around corners, spot what is hidden in plain sight, gain empathy for others and fresh insights on problems" (2021, xii). Anthropology offers an essential way of thinking and doing for solving issues; it provides a means for instigating change in the world to address the pressing issues today of climate change and the environment, respond to racism, social media overload, the rise of artificial intelligence, social inequalities, and political conflict. While we live in an age of artificial intelligence and data analytics that gather information on a large scale and offer rapid solutions to problems, data science presents a point of view that is incomplete, often narrowly focused, observed from a distance, and constructed by selecting its object of analysis through sets of parameters that typically reduce rather than expand issues. Business consultants, Christian Madsbjerg and Mikkel Rasmussen affirm, in *The Moment of Clarity* (2014), that most businesses create a linear mode of problem solving, using rational analysis, deductive reasoning and hypothesis testing in a quest to narrow and reduce complex variables. But this approach to problems fails to ask the larger strategic question of "why?"

The first premise of this book is to inform anthropology students, beginning practitioners and curious non-anthropologists about the ways in which anthropology provides an intellectual and practical framework for seeing and dealing with the larger "why"questions of human behavior in business and society. It shows ways of addressing issues holistically; identifying with people empathetically; acting reflexively and understanding situations from an emic, or insider's, point of view. Anthropology offers an expansive, open, and explorative way to "think ethnographically" (Hasbrouck 2018) through issues relevant to business, which can make a difference to society and the world. Using theories and tools from anthropology, this book hopes to introduce students to a different way of thinking about business strategy in a nonlinear way, to solve business problems, and help firms better understand human behavior.

A second premise of this book is to show the ways in which business anthropology advocates for change. An interventionist approach to solving problems explores how anthropological thinking and doing can be applied thoughtfully to the main areas of business anthropology: research in consumer markets, user experience (UX) and new business development; design concepts and strategies; and organizational work and work-culture environments, to bring about change. Each chapter provides multiple examples of anthropologists working collaboratively with others in these environments who have challenged corporate modes of thinking and revamped processes to be more responsive, adaptive and innovative towards their outward audiences and internal employees and shareholders. The intent is to demonstrate to students and practitioners how anthropology offers a powerful strategic and analytical framework for solving problems and fostering real change.

A third premise is to promote a "public anthropology" (Borofsky 2004) that addresses real social issues and problems beyond the discipline, and encourages broad, public conversations about them with the explicit goal of fostering social change. While many practicing anthropologists already do the kinds of things described as public anthropology, the term itself calls attention to the existing divisions between public/practicing applications and academic perceptions. The field of anthropology is being transformed by practice, that is, traditional academic anthropology applied outside of academia. Anthropological practice is now the norm. A united focus on public-oriented anthropology from all anthropologists would also help resolve the divide between academic and applied anthropology and join the discipline in popular appeal to address real social issues for broader audiences. Thus, the book hopes to provide academic scholars, practitioners, instructors, and students with a roadmap to integrate theory with practice, while advocating for real change in a public discourse, and it comes at an especially crucial time.

WHY IS THE FIELD OF PRACTICE AND BUSINESS ANTHROPOLOGY IMPORTANT TO STUDENTS TODAY?

In addition to myriad social and environmental issues facing society today, the field of anthropology is experiencing its own crisis. Elizabeth Briody, in her 2022 executive session at the American Anthropological Association (AAA) annual meeting, asserted that there is perhaps no greater concern among professional anthropologists and graduating anthropology students than that of employment. Numerous anthropology tracks at the AAA meeting sessions and other conferences in recent years discuss the employment crisis as an issue of academic precarity.[1] Traditional career paths of seeking out tenure-track jobs at PhD-granting institutions now only accommodate 10% of new PhD anthropologists, in addition to excluding MA, BA, and AD graduates. Yet, most academic anthropology programs in colleges and universities do not expose or prepare students for the range or diversity of careers outside of academia, particularly in industry, fields of design, nonprofit organizations, and government, where jobs are growing. This lack of exposure, in turn, reduces the number of anthropology students and jeopardizes anthropology programs, while weakening anthropology's public impact in the world. This is a time when all anthropologists should be a major voice in the world, taking the public stage and rallying for action. Although the AAA recognizes the importance of practice in anthropology, many anthropology programs in colleges and universities have been lax in responding. Many instructors say they do not know how to integrate teaching, practice, and application into their coursework and are unfamiliar with practitioner scholarship, and so they believe they do not know how to help students prepare for jobs beyond the academy. This book addresses this issue by bringing to the fore both scholarship on anthropological ideas and theory, and their application in practical, social, and commercial problems encountered in consumer research, business design and organizational worlds.

What has been needed and is lacking is a basic book that offers both ideas and examples of doing practice, using cultural analysis, while explaining the theoretical ways to analyze and interpret practice. The discipline of anthropology consists largely of practitioners employed in, or who consult for, a range of organizations, including for-profit and nonprofit organizations, financial corporations, small and medium scale businesses, family run businesses, government agencies, military organizations, financial institutions, educational institutions, labor unions, indigenous organizations, virtual and digital organizations, and healthcare and medical organizations. These career options are exciting and available to anthropology students, if they know how to apply their unique skill set to those careers.

Business anthropologists importantly differentiate themselves from other non-anthropological researchers. Other consumer researchers may claim to be ethnographic by stressing "being there," but read consumer behavior directly, elevating what consumers say or what is observed without a subsequent level of interpretation in analysis. Failing to situate and interpret consumer behavior and discourse within theoretical constructs simply highlights interesting moments in consumer research but lacks the potential for strategic analysis at a higher level, or comparative analysis of consumer behaviors in other situations or at other times. For instance, Paco Underhill, in a popular business book, *Why We Buy* (2008), uses basic observational approaches that are valuable, but anthropologists typically produce deeper understanding and insights. Anthropologists know that observation alone is limited because people often over- or under-report their actual behaviors, reframe their thoughts or say different things in different contexts. The interpretation of what is being observed and said (or not said) in a particular setting may help to understand power differences and gender roles by noting who is speaking and who is silent, noting relationships and differences with other people, and interpreting the use of material artifacts and their importance to a setting. Interpreting these "webs of significance" (Geertz 2000) requires a theoretical understanding of what to observe, what gender relations, social hierarchies, and forms of resistance reveal, what things mean to people, and how meaning changes in the different environments of home, shopping venues, corporate settings, or in design studios. This book offers such a perspective—where theoretically informed ideas and applied practices participate in a new scholarship and contribute to the development of theories, where research contexts and theoretical ideas for solving issues evolve in relation to each other, not as distinct and separate fields of inquiry. For readers familiar with practice and for business anthropologists this may seem plausible, while, for others in academia, the ideas here may be novel. The book offers ideas for all seeking to know more about a theoretically informed guide to anthropological practice.

WHAT DOES ANTHROPOLOGY OFFER STUDENTS AND BUSINESS PRACTITIONERS?

As this book hopes to reveal, there are numerous points of inter-section between anthropology and business, where thinking with anthropologically informed ideas and methods can lead to insights and opportunities that benefit business as well as society. An anthropological way of looking at social and human problems dovetails with business very well. Such ways of thinking and doing can intervene to guide and help organizations become increasingly effective as they come to understand, appreciate, and learn to work within their organizational cultures. Anthropologists can help organizations become more socially responsible and aware of their own internal cultures, and external outreach and messaging because business anthropologists, like practitioners generally, are *problem solvers*. They are focused on trying to address one or more issues so that organizations and what they produce and do is better for all stakeholders. Anthropologists accomplish this through reflexive thought, applying holistic perspectives, emic considera-tions, and longitudinal viewpoints, which help to transform busi-ness problems into human concerns of greater significance.

For instance, anthropologists looking at the "other," whether indigenous populations in the Amazon rainforest or employees of Amazon commercial warehouses, are trained to be self-reflexive about their own conclusions, values, work, and impact in the world. This is essential to ethnographic work, since a self-reflexive stance helps businesses properly understand what else they and others are experiencing in the world; it provides a comparative way of looking at things. This stems from two bases. First, this stance is epistemological, that is, a way of knowing the world. Through self-reflection, anthropologists gain a better under-standing of the strengths and limits of their own thinking and actions. Second, reflexive thought is ethical because anthropologists want to know the impact they are having on other people's lives, both positive and negative, and the effect they are having on related systems and society at large. It is by experiencing "otherness" that we can put ourselves in a position to consider culture from another perspective. As an example, this perspective is essential to design anthropology, for, as Adam Drazin (2021, 63) mentions, design creates an intrinsic "otherness" in its perspective, since seeing an object only in terms of its design makes sense because there is an attempt to consider or anticipate an other person, community or place who will use and appreciate it. This is done in an effort to make (positive) change on behalf of others.

Yet, this methodological approach of thinking thoughtfully and reflexively of others stands in contrast to what most businesses are taught. The standard way of thinking through business issues is linear, sequential, and progressive; it's about getting things done, moving forward and moving on. "Default thinking," as Madsbjerg and Rassmussen (2014) describe it, is a linear and rational mode of problem solving in business. It's successful at analyzing information extrapolated from a known set of data, and is popular because it creates efficiencies, optimizes resources, balances product portfolios, and cuts operational complexity. Business is about taking resolute action and not looking back, especially for the start-up mentality of disruption, acting fast and "breaking" things.[2] But what happens when the challenge involves understanding people's complex behavior? Anthropological thinking encourages businesses to reflect on themselves, to value consideration, and not just take determined and resolute action. In fact, it is through reflexive thought that new insights arise, and business may uncover new opportunities.

In addition to a reflexive perspective, holistic–systemic thinking—the ability to see the integrated picture, to pull back from the specific problem, event, or situation under study and put it in a larger context—is one of anthropology's most important contributions to business. A holistic approach considers how the parts to an organization are mutually influential and interconnected to other parts, larger processes, and whole networks; if one part is tweaked, then the effect ripples out to affect the rest of the system. Just as we understand culture as an integrated system, we can understand how issues are frequently integrated with other issues, so that to understand museum attendance, for example, one must look at use of space, types of visitors, and placement of objects, not just museum attendance. Sieck and McNamara (2016) discuss how holism reframes and expands conversation. For example, police violence could be reframed by viewing officer training as a ritual, or a police department as a kin network. In this way, you are "joining up the dots between different parts of people's lives" (Tett 2015, 133).

Many business organizations, in contrast, are taught to think and work as isolated parts rather than interconnected systems. Owing to theories of scientific management, many companies are organized into silos, which helps businesspeople get work done and keeps members of a particular functional specialty together. Individuals in a company work on specific projects and it gives people a clear idea of the task at hand, and what they are supposed to do. However, fractionalized thinking also prevents businesses from seeing the bigger picture, asking difficult questions, and understanding how one piece of work is creating a system that is unsustainable, and may have an impact on others, of which they are unaware.

From an opportunity-focused perspective, how can businesses spend more time learning the ways that all the pieces fit together, and how can what a business does fit into the larger economy? Anthropological ways of using cultural analysis reveal new opportunities to make an impact that businesses didn't even know were connected. In marketing, design, and innovation, for instance, business often focuses on the individual, rather than collective, activities of people to understand customer wants and desires, own that piece of their lives, and satisfy that need. This psychological perspective assumes that personality traits guide consumer motivation, decisions, and behavior, ignoring patterns of behavior that result from shared cultural values and trends. This perspective loses focus on a holistic and cultural understanding that people live among other human beings, who live and interact in various communities in relation to other people.

Anthropological ways of thinking also inform us of two perspectives of knowing: etic and emic. Etic is the formal, rational, and logical way of knowing things that most businesses implement. It is witnessed in formal knowledge that is passed on and shared in spreadsheets, data points, or marketing plans. It is also witnessed in language that a business uses to understand and evaluate its object. For instance, in the language of marketing, strategies are planned out in marketing campaigns, capturing market share, stealing target customers, defending positions, aiming at customers with big data, and considering customers as "revenue streams," as if they were natural resources to exploit. Not only does marketing language reflect a "war metaphor" that antagonizes and depersonalizes customers and competitors as the enemy, it also affects how marketers see other human beings.[3]

In contrast, an emic way of thinking about people is a local, informal way of understanding viewpoints and knowing things. From a business perspective, to understand an emic way is to understand how people frame value in their lives, addressing their concerns by showing empathy. This will help the business better connect with the challenges of their lives from understanding how people make sense of their lives.

For example, Madsbjerg and Rasmussen (2014) applied emic and etic concepts to corporate work with Adidas, a global sports equipment and athletic shoe company. They wished to understand the rising yoga phenomena and address an odd marketing question: "Is yoga a sport?" From the corporate perspective, or etic framework, yoga was a sport and should be marketed to, as would any other sport category. The main goal in any sport is to win against competitors. However, Madsbjerg and Rasmussen's research into changing lifestyles from an up-close and emic perspective showed a different perspective. Women and men attended fitness centers to take yoga classes in packed class sessions, even as membership in local sports teams lagged. They understood that these people were attracted to yoga, not as a form of competition, but for its well-being and lifestyle benefits. This was an eye-opener for Adidas, and changed the way they developed a clothing line. Thus, an emic exploration of the way consumers think and act showed how an activity creates meaning and value in people's lives, and also warrants an exploration of the organizational models and etic structures that produced the terms of the problem within the company in the first place. When we bring etic and emic perspectives together, we learn how people feel about things and how their perceptions are framed by their values and what is important to them.

Another dimension of using anthropology to understand consumer experience is to take a longitudinal view of products, services, and their extended impact on society. Understanding experiences of consumers is framed anthropologically by knowing how a particular experience fits into the rest of life with other people, and across annual cycles, tacking back and forth between big picture and small picture, which involves a deeper extended understanding of consumers' lives. Business, in contrast, tends to think mainly in terms of short segments of consumer experience: the hair-care experience, the snacking experience, the beverage occasion, and then seeks to "own that moment," so that a brand can design the product or service for it, and beat the competition in that space. But because of this short-sightedness, business often fails to look at human experience longitudinally over time, which has consequences. The plastic soda bottle introduced in the 1960s and 1970s sought to own and indulge "the refreshment moment" by bringing to market the liberating ideas of portability, disposability, and screw-off caps. But what was never considered was the plastic bottle itself and the longer-term repercussions of where to place the plastic, later in the life cycle. This didn't become a crisis until later. Issues such as sustainability require a long-term view and anthropologists can help businesses consider the longer-term consequences of their actions in the present.

What sets apart business anthropologists from other forms of business research is asking these larger questions of why and exploring the ways of integrating both the thinking and doing of ethnography in a contemporary setting of consumer research, design concepts, and organizational practices. Sarah Pink and colleagues (Pink et al. 2017, 5) speak to this need for integration of practice and theory when they write:

> What is glaringly lacking is a larger and extensive discussion of how forms of applied, public and practiced scholarship contribute to the development of cultural and social theory, and vice versa: how abstract theoretical insights can provide concrete proposals, insights or solutions and understandings in concrete contexts of daily life and work.

Applying ethnographic research with thought-provoking examples is a way to bridge theory and practice to fill this void. This book offers such a bridge by underscoring the productive connection between anthropological ways of thinking and implementation in the study of consumer research, design concepts and practices, and organizational work culture examples. It hopes to be a valuable resource to students, scholars and practitioners who embrace a theoretically informed approach to the practice and thinking of anthropology for business.

***

The second premise of this book is to highlight the ways in which business anthropology advocates for change. Practitioners and academics are divided in this aspect by differing approaches to research and the sense of purpose and ethics regarding the outcomes of their studies. The key differentiator between academia and practice is that while academics offer a critical analysis of cultural situations, practicing anthropologists aim to *solve problems.*

Most academic anthropologists are theoretically concerned with the investigation of cultural phenomena. The focus of their research is to understand and highlight the richness of human diversity by exploring the dynamics of people and their local community. But they are also cautious of ethnocentrism, attend to apparent structures of power that enable or constrain people, and question forms of representation in modern and past social constructions. Owing to a historical legacy of aiding colonialism and Western expansion agendas, cultural anthropologists are cautious of being authoritative and conclusive, and so resolve to offer anthropology as an "enterprise of critique." As George Marcus (2010, 43–44n) explains, "Since the 1980s, much mainstream social-cultural anthropology has become a minor science … in which social problems are not solved or explained in holistic terms, but which is rather a medium where conflicts might be articulated in different registers." Other anthropologists eschew easy explanations and, like Anna Tsing in her work on Worlding projects, embrace "the uses of disorientation…" for us to "…consider how unstable, incomplete and misleading," her Worlding projects are (Tsing 2010, 63). Tim Ingold equivocally posits, "Anthropology doesn't tell you what you want to know; it unsettles the foundations of what you thought you knew already… so you may end up knowing less than when you started, but wiser" (2018, 107). As these statements suggest and Ulf Hannerz admits, anthropologists are careful to present life in "subtle shades of gray ..." but also "they sometimes struggle to explain their work to outsiders in easy terms" (in Tett 2021, 233).

Presenting critiques of social issues in ambiguous "subtle shades of gray" may highlight complex problems and suggest systemic issues in society, but also makes the clear and easy-to-follow discussion of issues to the public oblique. Moreover, the motive to critique but not act is based in the AAA "do no harm" code of ethics and discourages ready solutions. If anthropology holds that we should not directly intervene to solve problems, cannot offer simple explanations, and cannot "tell you what you want to know", then we should not wonder why (academic) anthropologists are absent from public debate on crucial social issues. Moreover, as Ulf Hannerz explains (in Tett 2021, 233), "People who become anthropologists often have an anti-establishment view, and after studying how power works in the political economy they may feel cynical and or angry as a result." Feeling cynical or angry at authority, institutions, and organizations is a less constructive way to make change happen than by getting involved.

SOLVING PROBLEMS BY TAKING ACTION

In contrast, many practitioners work in and for business, government, or non-profit enterprises, which call for straightforward solutions and actionable results that are easier to report. Anthropologists are attracted to practice because of employment opportunities but also to be able to make a difference in society by addressing real social problems. The change today for anthropologists taking positive action is dramatic. John Sherry, a long-time business anthropologist remarks on this amazing about-face by reflecting on the 1970s and 1980s when he first trained as an anthropologist: "I think it is safe to say that, in that era, the only reason one might study contemporary commerce would be to subvert it; the thought that one might improve it would be heretical" (2017, 45). Unlike academic colleagues who sometimes marginalize practicing anthropologists and disparage their work, practicing anthropologists apply anthropology's capacity for solving real world issues that are of interest to governments, non-profit companies and for-profit industries, expanding beyond the traditional academic focus on teaching and research. According to Shirley Fiske and Robert Wulff (2022, xiii), practicing anthropologists are "solving problems in the broad swath of organizations and entities facing 'real-world' decisions and actions." Their work is not only valued and useful but makes a difference by showing "knowledge in action," such as in the assessment of results, making policy choices and defining actual problems of humanity. Anthropologists are applying anthropological theories and insights to solve human problems, revealing the strategies and methods used and the concrete actions taken to ensure projects are beneficial. Below are instances of anthropologists working alongside government or with industry solving real problems and making a difference.

Adam Koons (2022) worked with the government in rural Afghanistan in 2008 on the problem of severe food insecurity experienced by the farmers. The drought and poor farming methods not only meant people did not have enough food but also caused an increase in illegal imported food from Pakistan and, worse, an increase in growing poppies for the illicit drug industry. His challenge was to figure out how to enable small scale farmers to revitalize wheat production. Koons proposed a project with USAID that provided accessible agricultural supplies – more seeds, fertilizers for 250,000 farmers and that also would provide income-generating opportunities for farm employees. He helped create a system of vouchers to be redeemed at agricultural supply depots and ensure ownership via 15% copay. This strategy integrated a community level approach, holistic relationships between beneficiaries, avoiding charity, and responding to Afghans' sense of pride and ownership. The project successfully provided beneficiaries with 297,000 vouchers at a 99.9% redemption rate, aiding 1.7 million family members, including 3,000 female-headed households. In total, he reached 341,301 farmers with farming aid. Food security was re-established while self-esteem and self-determination of farmers was maintained, avoiding a charity-oriented system.

In another example of successful intervention, Amanda Stronza (2022) visited an Amazonian community in Southeastern Peru for her dissertation work on the impact of tourism on local culture. Ecotourism was promoted as a collective venture between government, conservationists, and the business sector as a form of sustainable development. Her question was: how would a marriage of business and conservation work out? Amanda decided to partner with the project and not just observe as an academic. She acknowledged that her work would be biased, subjective, and uncertain in predicting an outcome. Still, she relished being a "culture broker," and helped the community by teaching them skills in photography to turn what they photographed into observed data. She was also privy to company records at Posada Amazonas. As an insider, she could access clientele, administration, and locals, working across sides to translate insights and understandings into actions. The company was successful in promoting and protecting culture and the environment with the help of an anthropologist. The financial returns, which generated 2 million in local income, were reinvested into conservation efforts, building a lodge, and prohibiting hunting, timber extraction and farming, and protecting three thousand hectares of pristine land. Both community and company showcased wildlife habitats and cultural traditions of working locally to achieve sustainable goals. This story of ecotourism success gained publicity in *The New York Times, The Economist*, and *National Geographic*.

My own work with a group of international hotels and the World Wildlife Fund (WWF) revealed how sensory strategies could mitigate food waste. In 2017, I was hired as a consultant by the WWF to propose and experiment with ideas for minimizing hotel food waste. Forty per cent of food is discarded in hotels while alternative ways of utilizing guest food go unrecognized. My objective was to create new awareness and suggest measures within the food distribution process of hotels to curb wastefulness. I interviewed chefs, hotel managers, kitchen workers and hotel guests about the hotel food experience. However, I encountered an unexpected dilemma: food is the primary means by which hotels market "hospitality" to their guests. Dining buffets popularly display an abundance of food choice to guests, yet they also represent the most wasteful format: guests typically over-sample food and overload plates, so surplus food is later discarded. How could the hospitality industry reduce or limit a pleasure that was promoted as a guest benefit? Nevertheless, I applied a sensory strategy to the dining experience to sublimate people into consuming less. Sensory strategies can subtly discourage guests from excess food: using heavier and/or wide rimmed plates set kinesthetic and visual boundaries; food cooked in front of guests enhances enjoyment while reducing excess. These and other tactics help mitigate food waste and limit surfeit, while not interfering with the marketing dictum of hospitality that attracts guests. Initial results of a pilot study showed a 15% reduction in food waste[4] that is still being carried out. More research is needed to craft food experience journeys that appeal to consumers' concept of free choice, yet also help hotel management encourage moderation.

Solving problems in spheres of commerce, business and government is what distinguishes practicing anthropologists from their academic peers. Different ascribed goals between practicing and academic anthropologists and a general disagreement over anthropology's intentional and unintentional impact in the world furthers the divide, which also stems from different ethical interpretations of anthropological actions and considerations for appropriate behavior. Moreover, the central AAA code of ethics, "do no harm," creates serious complications in determining what is and is not "harm" since levels of engagement, area of focus, scope of work and evaluation of results differ greatly between practicing and academic anthropologists.

As a result of past and present behavior from anthropologists, the call to action and sense of purpose for practitioners and academic anthropologists are quite different: while the academically inclined AAA code of "do no harm" dissuades anthropologists from involvement, the call to "do some good" encourages practitioner anthropologists to take action.

MOVING PAST "DO NO HARM"

Academic anthropologists are perhaps hesitant to act and gain public recognition because their career field discourages seeking public attention, from a negative legacy of controversies that still haunts the discipline. The academic focus on publishing in peer-reviewed journals for tenure promotion and career advancement devalues easy communication to broad audiences, and, in fact, publishing articles aimed at the general public may even count against candidates (Sabloff 2011, 411). Moreover, if anthropologists wish to "make an impact" in the public sphere they are unfortunately better remembered for "behaving badly" (Mitchell 2014). Three recent incidents of anthropologists "behaving badly" created shockwaves in the anthropological community and brought bad press to anthropology. The controversies prompted the AAA to reassess its ethics standard and subsequently revise its ethics code to "do no harm." This action has been translated into a call for *inaction* as discussed by Jon Mitchell (2014) in his article on social impact and the politics of evaluation.

First, Napoleon Chagnon and James Neel's research on the Yanomami of Amazonia in 2000 sparked the *Darkness in El Dorado* controversy, in which a journalist accused the anthropologist and geneticist of causing a measles epidemic and exacerbating intra-ethnic violence among the community. While Neel and Chagnon were exonerated of the former charge, the latter remains debatable in terms of intellectual politics. The second incident is the "Human Terrain" program of the US military, embedding anthropologists within Iraq and Afghanistan from 2005 to 2007, which supporters claim reduced the need for counterinsurgency, but other anthropologists (Ferguson 2013, Sahlins 2013) saw as a manipulation of anthropology to assist in identifying military targets. Moreover, they argued, it threatened the safety of other anthropologists who might be falsely identified with the military. The third case is Anastasia Karakasidou's research in Greek Macedonia, in which she identified a Macedonian Slav minority, but which prompted threats of violence and retaliation against her and her publisher from Greek nationalists and caused the ultimate withdrawal of her book, *Fields of Wheat, Hills of Blood* (1997) from Cambridge University Press (later published by the University of Chicago Press).

In 2012, the AAA responded to these widely publicized and debated actions of anthropologists by developing a code of ethics[5] that calls for all anthropologists to follow its guidelines. However, the ethical responsibilities outlined in the code—doing no harm, obtaining informed consent, maintaining subjects' anonymity, and making the results of the research accessible—are responsibilities that may not apply to all anthropologists, especially considering the differences in practicing and academic fields.

WHAT ARE APPROPRIATE ETHICS FOR ANTHROPOLOGISTS TO FOLLOW?

Ethics are constantly changing and being updated. They reflect an ongoing process of awareness, reaction, interpretation and adaptation.

Former AAA President Monica Heller writes: "… our ideas about something are always developed in interaction with other people and in connection to our experiences" (Heller 2016, 231). Indeed, the AAA has been engaged in specifying, and subsequently revising, its code of ethics at least since 1967. Many anthropology associations, such as the National Association for the Practice of Anthropology (NAPA), the Society for Applied Anthropology and the Society for American Archaeology, have developed and continually revise their own ethical statements or standards of conduct to assist their members. In all cases, educating anthropologists on ethical behavior is not about proclaiming a set of hard rules and regulations on what should be ethical behavior. Rather, it's about "socializing students into habits of reflection and cultivating their sensitivity to the competing, often mutually contradictory needs and interests of multiple stakeholders."[6] Responsibility is then shifted to anthropologists to make their own best-informed decisions.

Ethical responsibilities also vary by anthropological practice. For instance, Maryann McCabe and Rita Denny (2019) discuss the current guiding principles in consumer research when working with clients, which include:

> protection of research participants through informed consent and confidentiality; accurate representation of research participants which, as Sunderland and Denny (2007) maintained, entails an understanding of the cultural dynamics at play in any situation including the dynamics of power; respect for contractual arrangements with clients such as non-disclosure agreements and good faith estimates of time and cost for conducting ethnography and cultural analysis; and selection of projects since business anthropologists may accept or reject work based on their judgment that a product is harmful to those who would consume it.

In reality, businesses, government agencies and non-profit firms, not anthropologists, are the agents actively shaping the world of commerce, politics, and exchange and its impact on society. Many practicing anthropologists desire to "do some good" and be part of the "agents of change" that determine the quality of our lives. Perhaps, this calls for a moral obligation for anthropologists to engage the world of policy making, commerce and economic activity by "doing some good." Now is the time for all anthropologists to engage in relevant social and environmental issues and drive change.

DOING SOME GOOD INVITES *ALL* ANTHROPOLOGISTS

Practicing anthropology is driven by challenges in myriad fields of engagement and seeks to make interventions that solve problems and have a positive impact in society. Briody and Pester (2017, 39) affirm that, "(practitioners) are working inside some cultural system—whether as employees, contractors, consultants, or even volunteers—and trying to make it better in some way." Solving problems with real social impact can inspire not just practitioners but all anthropologists. The following ideas suggest further ways that anthropologists can achieve positive outcomes and publicly acknowledge their actions by doing some good.

First, reflecting on the previously mentioned Neel and Chagnon crisis, Robert Borofsky (2018) writes, what if, instead of the AAA unsuccessfully trying to reprimand them for their actions and trying to determine the degree of harm,[7] the investigating committee insisted that the Yanomami people *benefit* from the research they conducted. This benefit might take the form of gift exchange.

Kadija Ferryman (2017) provokes us to think of collecting data as a form of gift exchange that works towards a common good. Data, she writes, is not a thing or a repository of information, but an action. Ferryman suggests researchers have an obligation to reciprocate when data is taken from a community, just as a gift is connected to actions of giving, receiving, and reciprocating. She says scientists missed an opportunity when they collected genetic data from indigenous communities to map human genetic diversity. The communities felt a lack of involvement during the research phase and saw it as an extraction of their biological resources. The scientists only saw data as information. But, if we reframe data as a gift, genetic data could be given back, such as in research on diabetes, helping the community beyond the scope of consent. This would show that practitioners are engaged in exchanges with employees, consumers, leaders, and users. Their findings and recommendations would be shared with those who hired them, so everyone benefits. This does not typically happen with academic anthropologists who write mainly for other anthropologists, and not usually for the communities they did fieldwork with.

Second, anthropologists can "do some good" when they work collaboratively with others towards the same goals. Rarely do anthropologists who work alone have the power to bring about significant social change. Unfortunately, this "solo" approach is identified with academic fieldwork, and for dissertations, is considered a rite of passage. To be effective, anthropologists need the energy and momentum generated by other people and organizations to mobilize people and persist through time. Anthropology works best when it collaborates with others to facilitate a common goal.

For instance, Robert Borofsky (2018) discusses how Partners in Health demonstrates ways to partner with local communities to build medical support structures on a community's existing structures, using community personnel for its medical support staff. Ulf Hannerz (2021) describes the Data and Society Group in New York using anthropology to study cyberspace, and Microsoft working with anthropologists to expose and remedy the plight of "ghost workers." John Sherry (2017) describes long-term collaborations with IDEO, a design and innovation consulting firm that delivers breakthrough interventions across industries and sectors. IDEO officers have written on the subject of the firm's methods and procedures to address research ethics that includes reflexive commentary on their design principles. Sherry (2017) also collaborated with Motorola, a global mobile communications firm that, through its Mobility Foundation, fosters community engagement across a range of stakeholders. The company has published an interdisciplinary collection of cases and commentaries on the ethical challenges it has faced around the world.

Finally, anthropologists in academia can do some good by teaching students about business anthropology and the broader field of practice, either as instructors in business schools, design schools or even in traditional anthropology classes. Teaching anthropological sensibilities applied to business reminds us that the power of change and impact to influence the world exists with business and commerce more so than it does with anthropologists. Therefore, preparing future business managers, marketers, designers, engineers, and anthropologists to enter the workforce with anthropology in mind, helps them to see themselves as moral agents, not merely passive observers. Students learn anthropological and ethnographic perspectives applicable to their vocation, as well as the ethical implications those perspectives bring to personal, organizational, social, and cultural spheres they inhabit. Students will go on to become influential corporate decision makers, public policy makers, urban planners, designers, engineers, marketers, and disciplinary thought leaders of heightened ethical sensitivity. They understand that, as corporate leaders, they can shape the quality of life in society, given that "marketing is among the most powerful forces of cultural stability and change at work around the globe, and accept that every marketing decision has a moral dimension" (Sherry 2017, 48). As they influence firms and help promote their brands, products and services to consumers, they will have the potential to realize the common good.

***

A third premise of this book is to encourage a more public-oriented anthropology to help solve social issues and help resolve the divide between academic and applied anthropology. Importantly, public anthropology addresses social issues and problems beyond the discipline, and encourages broad, public conversations about them with the explicit goal of fostering social change. A united discipline would appeal to a broader range of audience members, addressing particular issues and generating a public goodwill, that would also address the common refrain: Where is anthropology in the public arena?

This is one of the main rallying cries heard in academic conferences, anthropology meetings, in anthropology newsletters and at other venues. If anthropology is so valuable in its outlook on humanity and its take on social issues, why doesn't it hold a more prominent presence in public discourse for debating social issues? Tim Ingold, in *Anthropology: Why It Matters* (2018, 106), expresses exasperation:

> No other discipline is so pivotally positioned to bring to bear the weight of human experience in every sphere of life, on questions of how to forge a world fit for coming generations to inhabit. Yet in public debates on these questions anthropologists are for the most part conspicuous by their absence ... where are the anthropologists?

A collective focus on a public-oriented anthropology would help solve social issues and resolve the divide between academic and applied anthropology. Many of the outspoken public anthropologists of today are successful *practicing and academic* anthropologists. Creating public awareness and attracting media attention is a powerful way to bring the work of all anthropologists together in academia and industry, collaborating towards a common cause of supporting cultural knowledge and addressing timely issues. Anthropologists Elizabeth Briody and colleagues (2023), assert that more anthropologists need to step forward to inform audiences since the public and the media are hungry to learn about anthropology, as a way to know themselves better through history, actions, and the future, especially in the area of public interest in human behavior and culture. They claim local media outlets are often short of original content, and compelling stories can bring to life anthropological fieldwork, theory, and insight. Anthropologists who become public speakers gain competence and strength in learning how to communicate familiar anthropological ideas in unfamiliar ways to new audiences. Anthropology professor and futurist Genevieve Bell found that making anthropology's compelling insights "manageable, meaningful, and actionable" to a "totally different crowd of people" made her "a better anthropologist" (quoted in Briody et al. 2023) For Bell, it meant learning to communicate to tech companies, policy groups, and government as well as other academic disciplines. Here are some other examples.

DOING SOME GOOD FOR THE PUBLIC GREATER GOOD

Creating stories for media that have a compelling message with a specific goal in mind can connect directly with wide audiences. Helen Fisher is a TED Talk all-star. She bridges academics and practice as a biological anthropologist at Rutgers University and senior research fellow at The Kinsey Institute, Indiana University and is the most referenced popular scholar in the love research community. Fisher gains media attention as the leading expert on the biology of love and attraction. In fact, in 2005 she was hired by match.com to help build chemistry.com, which used her research and experience to create both hormone-based and personality-based matching systems. She has spoken frequently at TED conferences and is featured in an ABC News 20/20 special story on romance and attraction.

Anthropologists can also gain positive public awareness when they highlight issues through vivid comparisons. Comparison was once central to anthropology, yet many scholars have stepped away from it due to concerns over reductionism and oversimplification. But, as James Peacock (2002) counters, the global world offers myriad opportunities for comparison, and comparisons by anthropologists can make issues more relevant to the public because it also invites action. Academic anthropologists may have gotten away from comparisons because of their focus on globalization, which emphasizes flows and continuous interactions without boundaries (Appadurai 1996). Peacock writes that greater impact can be made, however, through informal comparisons, such as through anecdotes, parables, stories of people and their tendencies, which also gain public interest.

Another way to capture public attention is for anthropologists working in business to compare their work with other scholars studying the same business, or compare work across other cultures, whether applying theoretical topics to a study of a brand community, a hot topic on X (formerly Twitter), or a family-run business. For instance, Brian Moeran (2014, 80) ponders what the analogies are between North Italian silk manufacturing family firms and family-owned restaurants of Chinatown in London. How do they compare with each other and with the ideals of Japanese corporate "familism?"[8] Or what are the analogies to be made, for instance, between cult brands and current brands and the communities they represent. Saab and Harley-Davidson's online sites offer strong brand communities whose members tend to share more rituals, history, and tradition when compared with less cultish brands, such as Ford or Toyota. Their rituals and traditions take forms in greeting rituals, coded language associated with the brand community, celebration of special events and member milestones, sharing the history of the brand, and brand stories (Muniz and O'Guinn 2001). Applying anthropological theories to modern day ritualized communities lets anthropologists address the "why" questions of strategic importance for corporations. Anthropologists can also build off such comparisons to help the public better understand similarities and differences in family run businesses or online community formations among brands in the world around them.

Anthropologists can also attract attention by writing for broader audiences in accessible styles that intrigue with stories of impact. The public's attention may be captured in compelling stories, suggests Brian Moeran (2012, 52), by recontextualizing age-old anthropological theories of gift giving, magic, totemism, social dramas, and so forth in modern business case studies, as a way of making the strange familiar, and familiar strange. For instance, Horace Miner published an intriguing article in the 1950s titled "Body Rituals Among the Nacirema," which parodied American culture as an exotic tribe with odd rituals. More recently, Brian Moeran and I (Moeran and Malefyt 2018) have argued that certain industries depend on magic to sustain their businesses. Especially in the fields of advertising, fashion, financial predictions, the gaming industry, and the stock market, among other modern institutions, magical enactments guided by a magician, a rite and a formula (spell), offer a means to assuage fear, mitigate risk and reduce uncertainty by casting an enchantment of transformation over the process to assure success.

Similarly, anthropologists gain media attention by offering provocative responses to topical cultural issues, leading with a "hook." Anthropologist Suzan Erem[9] states, "the media isn't just out there running by itself. You have to reach out to them." What if an anthropologist told a reporter that "race doesn't exist," at least from a biological viewpoint. This might grab media attention with a follow up that would then discuss differences in skin color. Media could learn that race is a social concept, and not part of our DNA. Large-scale studies of skin pigmentation show that humans with both light and dark skin pigmentation have co-existed for hundreds of thousands of years. By making it interesting, anthropologists can turn it into a news story.

When questioning why the public doesn't listen to anthropology today, we may look back and be inspired by historical figures in anthropology who did have a strong public voice. These academic stars all had an applied focus and practiced engagement in the world, as they also suggested solutions for social change. The public was informed and influenced by anthropology because these anthropologists addressed topical issues important to public discussion and supported their work in the applied projects that they were involved in. Margaret Mead elevated discussions and enlightened the

American public by her work in Samoa (1928) and New Guinea (1930) on adolescent behavior and maturation, which led to improved social policies in the US. Ruth Benedict was active against racism in the 1940s. Her book, *Race: Science and Politics* (1940), refuted the then current theories of racial superiority and was used widely for teaching race and racism. Later, she developed a public affairs pamphlet for the basis of a children's book, cartoon-movie, and comic book. Bronislaw Malinowski (1926, 1927) contrasted Trobriand cultural practices with European norms, questioning and challenging the leading psychological applications of the Oedipus complex, and Gregory Bateson and colleagues (1963) compared schismogenesis with Western ideas of schizophrenia, which had a significant impact on psychiatry via his double-bind hypothesis. It wasn't just that these central figures were eloquent or compelling speakers; it was in part the way their material was presented in powerful stories of applied work that gained legitimacy for anthropology in the public sphere.

HOW DO ANTHROPOLOGISTS GET TO WORK IN INDUSTRY, BUSINESS, DESIGN FIRMS?

One of the goals of this book is to inspire anthropology and business students to work in fulfilling careers in industry. Many decide to transfer from academia to industry or from BA, BS or MA degrees into research jobs. Since opportunities for permanent employment in academia and tenure track positions are becoming increasingly scarce, more students are making the move to business. Especially now, industry offers many choices in the healthcare and technology sectors, marketing and user experience, design and organizational sectors. The challenge for anthropologists is to convince companies of the value of their anthropological skill set.

Anthropologist Nadine Levin (2019)[10] wrote a compelling article on her transition from academia to industry, where she currently works at Facebook. Her advice for transitioning to industry jobs also reflects many of the points discussed earlier in this introduction about differences between academia and industry. Understanding and applying these differences to job prospects is essential to knowing how to successfully transition from school or academia to a career in industry. Her collected words of advice are summarized here to help anyone who is thinking of transitioning from academia to industry.

When interviewing for a new job, anthropologists need to make an impact. This is done by translating academic skills and knowledge of anthropology into a language and style that industry people can understand. Translating anthropology skills into the language of the business world will vary, whether for UX, consumer research, organizational management, or design studies. Robert Morais and I discuss learning the language and codes of advertising to transition into marketing related careers (Morais and Malefyt 2010).

Levin advises students to learn to develop additional research methods beyond ethnography. For instance, her work in UX research is often best-fit and adaptive, which means using the best tool for the business and research question at hand. Sometimes, research questions are best answered with a quick survey, and, at other times, with exploratory ethnographic research. Many companies expect researchers to utilize a wide range of methods and approaches beyond ethnography. This means students should be prepared to learn new methods and to embrace a diversity of methods, in addition to ethnography. Other methods are described in the next chapter, on methodologies.

Along these lines, ethnography in industry is quite different from academic ethnography in that industry work needs to be practical, flexible, and fast. Turnaround time from planning to communicating results may take place over a two- to three-week period. And the field site for conducting observations and interviews in industry can be any in-context interaction—including the home, office setting, shopping in stores, or using a product in context, such as athletic equipment in a gym. This requires adaptation, while using the same principles as discussed in the methodology section of this book.

As pointed out earlier, industry jobs are most often collaborative, and success at work depends on one's ability to work with others. Teams of people work better than isolated individuals and can foster professional growth. At Facebook, Levin describes working alongside designers, engineers, and data scientists, where everyone collaborates towards a common problem and solution. Skills are needed, she says, to translate the substance and value of anthropological ideas and concepts, so that people with different backgrounds can understand it.

Along with this, networking with other people in industry is crucial. Sharing insights with colleagues and offering to help others on projects creates more opportunities for you. Moreover, working on teams and informing others about your work, why it matters, and why they should care, will help promote your work within the firm. Your ideas can also be promoted in different formats—reports, short presentations, videos—which are useful to different positions of employees. Projects are stories that can be told for inspiration and for impact to different audiences with different purposes.

Also, as mentioned throughout this book, industry research seeks to instigate change. Business anthropologists are expected to offer solutions, not just critiques of social issues. Beyond describing a study of a community or that the finding is inherently "important" in its theoretical finding, researchers need to articulate what resulting change the study made. This means identifying how the way people framed a problem changed, or how an organization pursued its key goals, or the ways in which a process, service, or product was developed or used.

Some colleges are starting to understand the importance of preparing students for the job market beyond the academy—as well as the value of the contributions that practitioners in private, public, and non-profit sectors are making to various disciplines. But progress is slow, and not all school programs or instructors are up to date. Therefore, reach out to a community of practice through in-person meetings, online meetups, and various websites that are designed for practitioners as a place to learn more about transitioning to industry.

STRUCTURE OF THE BOOK

This book introduces anthropology students, beginning practitioners and non-anthropologists to the range of approaches, concepts, and work practices in business anthropology that focus on the ways anthropologists address challenges and implement change. Chapters explore the major sub-fields of business anthropology, such as methodologies for business anthropologists; consumer research; design anthropology; organizational anthropology; and a concluding chapter on new directions in digital anthropology. Woven into each chapter are discussions on how anthropologists lead by example and address challenges, such as: gender and racial inequality, product and user experience innovation, and other examples of projects that help direct purposeful change. Anthropologists are also employed in fields of advanced technology, such as artificial intelligence, machine learning, and data science, leading new directions of practice. Examples of their work is given in the hope of inspiring students and generating greater public awareness of the ways anthropologists can address the most pressing social issues today.

Chapter 2, on methodologies in the anthropology of business, offers an introductory discussion on the value of carrying out cultural analysis, using ethnographic methods of participant observation and depth interviewing, and making the taken-for-granted in culture more visible. The chapter discusses how the process of discovery in research with consumers, user experience, or company employees is a co-created process and involves social collaboration between the interviewer, respondent(s), and context. Data are not revealed as much as they are "cooked" at every stage of the research process. It also discusses a range of methods and tools that business anthropologists employ, from traditional ethnographic methods of depth interviewing and participant observation to focus groups, projective tools, and mixed methods approaches. Along with discussions of methods relevant case study examples are presented that introduce students to the range of approaches needed to perform tasks in real-life situations, preparing students for careers in a range of industry related fields.

Chapter 3, on consumer research, presents an overview of anthropologists conducting consumer research in the fields of marketing and advertising, product development, market research, UX research, sustainable consumption, and cross-cultural consumer research. The focus of research in this chapter is to discover the manifest and hidden cultural meaning of products, brands, and services in the everyday lives of people, and report this information back to their corporate clients. And beyond representing the cultural meaning of products, brands, and services, anthropologists in consumer research interpret their discourses and observe patterns of behavior in cultural analysis that show human agency in creative and often unexpected ways. Conducting consumer research is shown as a process of discovery of the taken-for-granted dimensions of culture which becomes evident not only by being there in context with the consumer, but by partaking in their actions. Being "in" the experiences of others in cultural analysis of consumer contexts not only reveals unexpected insights for clients, but can create positive change in products and services, and the world at large.

Chapter 4 deals with organizational anthropology, and focuses on understanding the cultural and social dimensions of work culture and how they shape, and are shaped by, cultural practices within an organization. Anthropologists who study organizations approach the subject from a holistic perspective, considering the various cultural and social factors that influence organizational behavior and practices of individuals and groups at all levels, from top to bottom. They aim to understand how organizations are embedded in, and shaped by, cultural norms, values, beliefs, and power dynamics. Anthropologists in organizations investigate the importance of cultural factors in shaping organizational practices and outcomes and examine power dynamics and the ways in which power is exercised, negotiated, and flows within organizations. Overall, the focus of this chapter offers valuable insights into the complex and dynamic nature of culture in organizations and its role in shaping and being shaped by the wider cultural and social context.

Chapter 5, on the subject of design anthropology, details an interdisciplinary field that combines principles from anthropology and design to study human behavior and culture that inform the design process. To design is to conceive of an idea, plan it out, give form, structure and function before carrying it out in the world. In other words, design is creating with intention. Design research helps inform the design of products, services, and environments to better meet people's needs and desires. Design anthropology also uses theories in anthropology to assess the social nature of designed products and services with the aim to create designs that are culturally and socially sensitive, and that consider the human experience and context in which they will be used. This leads to developing more meaningful and impactful designs that have a positive effect on people's lives. Examples of design anthropology in this chapter can be seen in the design of technology products, such as smartphones, as well as in the design of physical environments, such as homes, workplaces, and public spaces.

Finally, Chapter 6, on digital anthropology, explores new ventures in understanding the complexity of human activity in the new digital environments of artificial intelligence, machine learning, and data science. This chapter examines recent trends of innovative anthropologists in their work of addressing social issues, as they forecast new directions in promoting online art communities, stopping hate groups, or exploring the current and future effects of teleport-robots, drones, and self-driving autonomous cars. Digital anthropology offers an exciting new field of academic scholarship and social practice for anthropologists to address the ways in which the digital, material, and social worlds are entangled in processes and products that have an impact on society. Moreover, ethnographic methods in digital technologies and collaboration with other data scientists in research opens the way for anthropologists to attend to current social concerns as well as future-oriented challenges that new technologies present. Anthropologists are directing the challenges that new technologies and digital futures bring, as they investigate digital technology in the communities, society, and the world we live in. In this way, anthropologists can and do make an impact in the public arena by addressing relevant social issues and showing anthropology's real contribution is in its capacity to transform lives.

NOTES

1 For example, see AAA session on transitioning from academia to industry: https://www.cultureofhealthtech.com/addressing-academic-precarity

2 See Facebook's founder Mark Zuckerberg: "Move fast and break things."

3 See Mark Chussil (2016), and Malefyt (2003) discusses the "war" metaphor used in an advertising workshop.

4 In 2018 Hilton adopted a pilot at hotels in Florida, Texas, and Columbia. Participating hotels reduced food waste by more than15% and donated more than 6,000 pounds of food, while keeping 260,000 pounds of food from landfills. https://wwf.exposure.co/usa-reducing-food-waste-in-hotels.

5 http://ethics.americananthro.org/

6 http://ethics.americananthro.org/

7 The AAA unsuccessfully tried to sanction Chagnon for his actions, rejected by a vote that involved less than 15% of the AAA's membership. The issue remains still in dispute.

8 See Chapter 4, on organizational anthropology, for discussion on consulting for small business enterprises in Italy.

9 Anthropologists on the Public Stage, Module 2; see www.anthrocurious. com

10 See also, Elisabeth Powell, 2019, 'Why Businesses and Consumers Need Us'.

METHODOLOGIES OF CULTURAL ANALYSIS

This book introduces the importance and value of anthropological thinking to business anthropology in its prime areas of consumer research, design concepts and user experience, and organizational work culture. Anthropological thinking comes from carrying out cultural analysis in the context of these areas. This chapter focuses on the methodological considerations and project implications that enliven the research process of doing cultural analysis.

The first part of this chapter discusses the advantages of applying cultural analysis and how it differs from popular psychological applications in several case studies. Ethnography is shown to illuminate the taken-for-granted aspects of culture and make the invisible visible, or, in anthropological parlance, make the familiar strange. This section covers the basics of ethnography, participant observation, and in-depth interviewing.

The second part of the chapter discusses various applied uses of cultural analysis. It covers a range of considerations for selecting the appropriate research approach and reviews the differences in approaches when seeking to answer a research question. This follows a discussion of different uses and applications of qualitative and quantitative research and the type of work projects they are adept at solving. This will provide an overview of a variety of research methods that are required in a range of fields for a successful career as a business anthropologist.

DOI: 10.4324/9781003358930-2

PART I: WHAT IS CULTURAL ANALYSIS? ORDERING AT-HOME PIZZA AS A FAMILY RITUAL

When I began my work at BBDO advertising as an in-house anthropologist doing consumer research for agency clients, one of my first big projects was to better understand the at-home pizza ordering process for a major pizza chain. The international pizza brand was one of our largest clients, so I was charged with making this right! As it turns out, it was one of my most challenging projects.

The client, a restaurant pizza chain, was aggressively pushing into home delivery service and sought a competitive edge by using ethnographic research to better understand in-home pizza consumption. From my study we would develop strategic ideas for advertising. The project appeared ethnographic at its core: research in multiple US locations, lengthy in-home interviews, ordering and discussing pizza with the family present, charging respondents to fill out extended diaries about pizza delivery, along with collage work of how pizza plays a role in their lives. The difficulty lay, however, in the structure of the research project: it was highly psychological, not anthropological.

To begin with, the client had previously developed the consumer target for the study: US mothers of families who wanted to order pizza for home delivery. The client had further segmented these target mothers into psychological "types," identified from a previous psychological study. The client insisted on using these preset psychological profiles, as my research was to determine how mothers planned and ordered pizza differently for their families according to these two profiles. Consumers were categorized into either "pressure cooker" or "night-off" moms, which were developed from a set of personal drivers and psychological responses to life issues. Pressure cooker moms were characterized as type A personalities, who led stressful, busy lives, always "under pressure," and needed last minute meal ideas for their families. For quick dinner solutions, speed of delivery service and efficiency were prioritized to "ease her tensions." The night-off mothers were characterized more as Type B personalities by their desire or "need" to plan a more relaxing occasion for the family, to gather and enjoy a meal together; quality of experience was prioritized. My assignment was to discover marketing ideas for each customer segment.

In addition, the nature of the questions that the client wanted answered were also highly psychological. Questions centered on researching how "night-off" moms differ from "pressure cooker" moms. The questions I was to research revolved around exploring and discovering the "unmet needs" of each consumer segment. These questions framed an individualistic response to my research questions. I attempted to reframe the research questions more culturally as: What is pizza? How is pizza different from other types of food people eat or order from restaurants, or expect from delivery? Under what types of conditions do mothers order pizza and what happens when pizza arrives at the door and is consumed by the family?

I argued with the client that a mom could experience either or both mood states depending on conditions, and that the same person might desire a casual planned-out dinner for one occasion and a hurried pizza for another. I suggested that understanding the cultural meanings—not the psychological meanings—of the conditions under which she might order pizza was both the key temporal question facing the brand and a more appropriate use of ethnography. The client, however, remained obstinate in uncovering how mom "types" were different as people.[1]

In the case of the pressure cooker moms or night-off moms, the salient cultural issues of exploring the meaning of domains such as work, play, meals and family togetherness, were overlooked. The client was less interested in the shared values and meanings of "pizza time" for the family in today's world. I had to acquiesce and rewrite my findings according to the psychological "buckets" the client had predetermined. While I was able to reframe cultural issues in terms of ritualized family "need" for togetherness—which pizza time represented—these culturally relevant ideas comprised only a small portion of the final report, while a larger portion was dedicated to discussing the psychological similarities and differences between mom types and issues that revolved around satisfying needs for "the self."

WHAT MAKES CULTURAL ANALYSIS SO UNIQUE?

As this example suggests, the analytic focus on the individual pervades our (US) society and assumes much effort from business anthropologists in analysis of organizational work-culture practices, design research, concepts and user experience, and especially consumer research for marketing, branding, and advertising purposes. From the widespread parlance of Type A personalities, introvert, extrovert, narcissist, over or underachiever, obsessive–compulsive character, to a range of terms that popularly make discussions, psychology has dominated political, business, and popular vocabulary. This psychographic perspective assumes that a set of developmental characteristics and innate personality traits direct individual motivations, and helps people make decisions, singularity guiding purchasing behavior. To see things through a psychological framework is the way most businesses look at things, from the use of Maslow's Hierarchy of Needs to the postmodern self.

Anthropology, in contrast, assumes a structure of shared meanings that gives coherence to our everyday lives. It seeks patterns of behavior that might result from shared cultural values and common belief systems. Culture, as a fluid construct of meanings, metaphors, ideas, and practices is made visible through individual action, but the meanings are inherently social and collective. Culture, then, is about the symbolic, practical (material), and relational aspects of everyday life that become, "apparent at the social level of observation …" and can be better understood as an organizing matrix of "ongoing human activities and meaning making," not as a thing or variable to be measured or validated in consumer research (Sunderland and Denny 2007, 49). Patricia Sunderland and Rita Denny exhort anthropologists in business to avoid the popular study of "culture" as a factor, condition, or "thing" to be investigated, such as of particular subgroups, like Early Adopters, Mexican Americans, or Urban Hipsters, which assumes an essentializing and measurable variable of culture that can be extracted, reduced and compared with other such measures.

Any focus on individual actors by anthropologists requires incorporating theories of human agency and power in sociocultural life, as well as acknowledging that culture is not static, situated and isolated in one place or time. Cultural processes and people are fluid and dynamic across place and time (Appadurai 1996) and show the ways in which human action and reaction in various contexts have an effect on others. This idea integrates with the concept of holism, that actions of individuals are not isolated but ripple out and affect other people, situations, ideas, practices, and so forth.

The process of doing ethnographic research, then, is not merely collecting data by gathering what people say or by singularly observing what they do "out there" in a particular context. Research information or data are not gathered so much as they are constructed, co-created, and produced. This means we don't just discover "raw insights" existing in some place in our observations, interviews, or by some other form of fact gathering. Rather, any process of discovery is really a co-created process, a *social collaboration* between the interviewer, respondent(s), and the "situated context" (Suchman 2011), which takes place at every stage of the research process: setting up the project, selecting respondents, using theoretical perspectives, applying various data gathering technologies and techniques of recording, which all have an impact and effect on what is ultimately constructed. As researchers, we, too, are part of the "cooking" process in the construction of answers we find to the questions we ask, explicitly and implicitly.

This also reveals the process of reflexivity by including our presence in research, which impacts the subject under study. We aren't detached observers, but part of the process, with our own biases. This is the essence of participant observation. Meaning isn't transparent or obvious, but embedded or hidden in cultural assumptions of what things mean and often goes unspoken, both for us and for our respondents. We therefore listen and look carefully for "invisible" cultural meanings, shared symbols and taken-for-granted categories and divisions that organize other people's and our own lives, and our clients' perceptions and actions.

In *Sorting Things Out,* Geoffrey Bowker and Susan Leigh Star explore classification systems in culture and emphasize the role of invisibility in the process by which classification orders human interaction into meaningful content. Selecting how the social world is categorized is always a cultural judgment, making relevant and visible those ambiguous features that are desirable, while making irrelevant and obscure other features that are less desirable (Bowker and Star 2000, 320). During apartheid in South Africa, for instance, a racial classification system played a key role in unjustly segregating the population based on physical characteristics.

Sunderland and Denny (2007, 48) reveal invisible aspects of culture while watching someone clean a floor in a client project for a floor cleaning product. They ask: What is a floor? What is clean? What is a cleaner? Rather than ask psychologically what the motivation is for keeping the house clean, anthropologists try to discern assumptions the person must have in order to clean the floor in a particular manner. We might also ask that person or ourselves: What does clean mean? What is different about a clean floor versus a clean table? This matters because, as Mary Douglas (2002) posits in *Purity and Danger*, what's clean and what's not demonstrates the contingent and socially determined nature of culture: people might cringe if someone placed shoes on a clean tabletop but not on a clean floor, because the former is not a "proper place" for shoes; hence, what is considered dirty is "matter out of place." The term "invisible" applies to these cultural meanings because items can be so familiar, embedded or tacit that neither the respondent nor the observer can initially discern their existence. Attempting to make the familiar, tacit, and the new (for instance, new ideas of what constitutes a clean floor) obvious is the task of cultural analysis. Indeed, making the familiar strange is what anthropologists are used to doing and offers an advantage of cultural analysis over psychological analysis. The task of making culture visible is a challenge because it is often simply taken-for-granted, as evident in the following story.

A STORY ABOUT AUTOMOBILE ENGINE OIL

Making culture visible in cultural analysis shows how asking a different set of questions challenges assumptions we hold. It revealed a cultural meaning of cars, which provided a deeper understanding of why some people are willing to spend twice as much for a synthetic motor oil over a conventional motor oil, when they change engine oil for their car.

As director of consumer insights at BBDO advertising, I was involved in leading an agency pitch for Mobile One synthetic motor oil. To win the advertising business for the brand, we had to show some fresh insights and a new understanding of their brand and an understanding of the category of motor oil for cars. I set out with a small team to investigate the deeper meaning of changing one's motor oil, specifically with the research question to address: why would a customer pay more for a synthetic motor oil over a conventional motor oil?

We broke down the target market for changing a car's motor oil into three different consumer experiences: taking your car to a dealership or independent service station for an oil change; taking it to a branded oil-change specialist (like Jiffylube); or doing it yourself at home. We visited all three locations in the New York, New Jersey, and Connecticut areas.

The background information we received from previous psychological motivation research on Mobile One was that it offered superior lasting protection for engines. The psychological insight for changing engine oil was that it lets people feel "in control," and gives them greater "assurance, confidence, peace of mind" when changing the oil. I wanted to study the practice from a cultural point of view.

An anthropological perspective can reveal consumer experience with motor oil in a different light, since cultural analysis poses a different set of questions. Rather than ask in interviews specifically about motor oil, such as what are qualities of a good motor oil, or how one feels when changing the car's motor oil (psychological motivations), my team asked a very basic cultural question: what is a car? This question seems so obvious and even dumb, but part of cultural analysis is making the hidden obvious.

Our question revealed that people's relationship with their cars runs deep. Cars in America evoke strong feelings from their owners. We learned about cultural practices, rituals, behaviors around cars. An "emic" or "insider" view of car owners revealed that owners treat their cars not as things, but as living personalities: cars are animate entities with feelings, agency, and actions of their own; cars are often given personal names; owners develop intimate relationships with cars and treat them as if they are members of the family. And most significantly, some people will pay double for synthetic oil since, we understood from the research, changing the oil lets owners feel they can "give back" for all their car does for them. The car as an animated entity gives something of itself in providing reliable daily service to the owner, and this action requires a reciprocal response of equal or greater measure as a gift in return, to keep the relationship going strong.

From this insight we developed advertising messages at BBDO that used the metaphoric language of "family" to imply that your car is part of your family. This offered Mobil One a new way for customers to relate to their car. Changing the car's engine oil gives back to your car for all the things it does for you, so it expresses care, like protecting a family member to keep the relationship happy and alive. In any event, we won the client's business with this insight.

***

Sometimes clients raise the issue concerning quality over quantity; how can so few interviews in an ethnographic study, such as 15 to 20 interviews, compare to a large survey, which might amass hundreds of interviews? Yet, we may respond, are we really measuring less? Fewer interviews still generate huge amounts of data. The time spent on a topic with an individual, circling back, getting a deeper, more complete answer provides a richness that is incomparable to any other type of data collection. Typically, we are also adding supplemental information such as photographs, diaries, collages, hand-written notes, direct observations, video logs, and other information, so the data is varied and deep.

In comparison, for example, surveys may quantify huge amounts of data but often less efficiently and are prone to false information. An airline survey may ask, "How many business air trips did you take last year?" Frequent travelers might then speculate every single time on a plane. How many trips are round trips? How many legs did I fly during each trip? What about mixing business with pleasure? With surveys, the answers are already provided by the researcher and the respondent must select from the provided answers, even if he/she has questions or comments. So, flyers typically guess because they cannot interact with the survey. An inaccurate survey still generates numbers, and the researchers are happy with numbers because they seem objective and complete.

While numbers can tell us the when, where, how much, and how often of human behavior, they fail to explain why. Cultural analysis of human action can help situate these numbers into a fuller, more descriptive social and cultural context. It can contextualize numbers in a narrative of the life of the person involved. How has the experience of parenthood changed over recent years and what is a family nowadays? What does "home" mean to the elderly moving into assisted living situations, or how does a single mother organize her time? Such questions are essential to the study of modern societies and are best answered by ethnographic approaches to research.

ETHNOGRAPHY AND PARTICIPANT OBSERVATION

Ethnography is the study of culture—or, more precisely, from the Greek, *ethno* or folk and *grapho* is writing, or more simply understood as the "writing about culture." Ethnography is not a singular approach to qualitative research but includes multiple methods, such as participant observation, videography, semiotic analysis, archival research, netnography, diaries, and collage work, among other techniques. Ethnography provides open, flexible, and adaptive contextual insights into the objects, people, products, and relationships that consumers are involved in. Sarah Pink and colleagues (Pink et al. 2016) argues that ethnography is best conceived and applied as an interpretive process in which a set of values are applied to researching people and culture. As Jay Hasbrouck (2018) posits, ethnography is a way of thinking, helping ethnographers develop a perspective for looking at culture, seeing what is taken-for-granted through active involvement in it.

Ethnography starts with observations and aims to offer a rich narrative account of a specific culture, allowing you to explore many different aspects of the group and setting. Ethnography strives to take the consumer, user, or employee's point of view. It gives the researcher direct access to the culture and practices of a group, and this "emic" point of view is useful for learning first-hand about the behavior and interactions of people within a particular context (see Ladner 2014). Geertz (2000) described ethnographic work as "thick description," in which participants are brought to life as intelligible, sympathetic protagonists in the details of the description of whatever they are doing. In our investigations, when we describe our consumers' or employees' actions using thick descriptions, they become key actors in our stories who carry the plot and unfold the drama as the central focus in our research. Detailing our informants' actions in stories is a way to personalize and interpret our descriptions to others. Jay Hasbrouck says stories are primary vehicles that "set contexts, indicate values, demonstrate flows of power, and signify intentions" (2018, 89). They help situate our thick descriptions in a familiar form of communication to others that humans respond to and regularly use. This approach of interpreting observations contrasts describing observations at face value. Paco Underhill (2008) observed shoppers in stores, as a result of which he famously described the "butt brush" effect. When shoppers approached sale items positioned near a store entrance but were brushed from behind by people passing in or out of the store, they abandoned shopping. Sam Ladner (2014, 120) calls this "non-reactive" or, simply, passive observational collection of data. Without interpretation of the context in which this occurred or interviews with shoppers about what happened, it is not ethnographic.

Geertz (2000) famously provided an example of ethnographic interpretation of a cultural event. A wink of an eye can mean different things depending on the context. From a behavioral observation, a wink from a character without interpretation could simply be described as a rapid downward movement of an eyelid, as Paco Underhill might observe. But a thick description interprets the whole event, characterizing the person's possible intentional and communicative meaning to others in the event. A wink can be complicit, seductive, friendly, sexual, patronizing, funny, even threatening. Without understanding the cultural context, a wink cannot easily be interpreted.

In addition to thick description, emic and etic approaches to qualitative research are what make ethnography so valuable to industry. An emic or "insider" viewpoint puts the research participant and his/her community in the center by focusing first on the context and the meaning of things to others within that context. Emic approaches to research seek to determine not only the insider use of categories, opinions, concepts, and language but also, importantly, what they mean to people within the particular context of the study, as a part of the research process. An emic way of understanding is to be aware of how issues frame consumers' lives, addressing concerns that also resonate with them, to help make sense of their lives. But we also need to know where a corporation is coming from, what their perspectives are, their concepts and categories, and how this frames an emic view to help foster change from within.

An etic perspective, in contrast, is the formal or standardized perspective that uses criteria external to the system. Elements of one system may be compared to and contrasted with another system because they are standardized. This is the way an expert or specialist would use formal terms or descriptions to describe what is going on. For example, an etic description might follow a doctor's diagnosis of a patient's illness in terms of symptoms, remedies for treatment, and hopeful prognosis. The formal and standardized language is useful and necessary to alert another doctor, in Mumbai for instance, if the patient travels, or if the doctor queries the procedure to follow in a similar patient diagnosis and needs to predict a prognosis as well. So, while doctors speak of patients' symptoms in an etic framework, patients speak about illness in terms of discomfort, pain, or fatigue, in an emic framework.

Research that delves into meaningful relationships of customers, their communities, values, and beliefs will show that both emic and etic understandings are valuable, since, when a misalignment of actions and values occurs, an anthropological view can help obviate where miscommunication occurs. Business anthropologists need to know both etic and emic perspectives, since learning how an individual or community might feel about a brand, how their perceptions are framed by their values and experiences with the brand, very likely differ from how the company thinks about and markets the brand experience.

By becoming immersed in a social environment, the anthropologist has access to more authentic information and spontaneously observes dynamics that would likely not have been available simply by asking on a survey. In this way, we understand the user experience from an emic perspective, from the participant's own language, concepts, categories, and opinions, which often modifies or adapts what corporations—an etic perspective—consider their product to be. Cultural analysis aims to discover the interrelationships between categories, not as isolates, but as entangled elements of culture, and how the categories are related to other categories.

THE BASIS OF PARTICIPANT OBSERVATION

Participant observation is the main qualitative research method in ethnography in which the researcher is immersed in the daily activities, practices, events, and relationships of her or his study population. Researchers use participant observation to gain a deep and broad understanding of sociocultural practices in their field sites by gathering data on both the mundane and the extraordinary in the everyday lives of research subjects. Participant observation is complemented by careful recording of activities, social actors, and spatial settings in the researcher's field notes, by camera, video recordings, and other data collection devices.

Business anthropologists' ethnographies differ from traditional ethnographic studies conducted by academic anthropologists in the shorter duration of time spent in observation, which may be several hours per interview over multiple settings. Academic anthropologists conventionally integrate into the life of the community they study over many months, even years, to develop an understanding of the community's world view, special events, and daily life that may change by season. Corporations operate under much shorter time frames. But, as Sarah Pink and colleagues (2016) notes, lengthy fieldwork may not even be desirable, or indicative of good ethnography, since observations in short time frames can provide substantial insights into consumer behavior.

The researcher participates as she observes to draw out patterns of social life, breaks in those patterns, and the often-contradictory relationship between cultural ideals (what people say they do) and practices (what people actually do). Because immersion with the respondent brings awareness and ideas both suddenly and gradually, either in one setting over time, or in multiple settings at different locations, participant observation is an iterative process. This means, the researcher expects the nature of and questions in ethnographic research to change during the project as feedback from consumers modifies the learning process. Fieldwork involves tacit knowledge and learning comes gradually and in spurts, but it *comes from doing.*

Sociologist Richard Sennett alerts us to the value of observing respondents engaged in the activity that we are investigating. While discussions about an activity are informative, watching consumers perform the activity elicits much richer data. Sennett believes that "Thinking and feeling are contained within the process of making" so that something like craftwork is undertaken because it is fulfilling in itself as an embodied experience (2008, 7). Additionally, "making physical things provides insight into the techniques of experience that can shape our dealings with others" (2008, 289). Critical to contextual observation is watching people do an activity. Research on cooking for Campbell's (detailed in

Chapter 3) revealed insights into the improvisational adaptations of mothers while cooking, which were very different from their after-the-fact reports of simply following a recipe. Improvising while cooking requires thoughtful care and concern about qualities, people the meal is for, and anticipated outcomes, so watching mothers adapt recipes to the preferences of individual family members showed a level of care *in action*. This was not reported in the customer cooking surveys that Campbell's had previously conducted. We saw, in context and from embodied action, how knowledge expressed in cooking movements and recollections fills the gaps of anticipated outcomes with improvisation.

Observation in ethnography is an important first skill in "noticing things" but cultural analysis based upon ethnography goes further than describing details: it offers explanation. Beyond a description of what is observed or what people say, anthropologists interpret what they observe and explain in cultural terms. Beyond merely documenting social life, anthropologists provide thoughtful interpretations drawn from theoretical understandings about its meaning. As patterns become apparent in descriptions, anthropologists seek to interpret these patterns into some coherent and meaningful story about our participants.

Making visible the care of improvisation in cooking is another way of making the familiar strange in research. Taking familiar consumer categories such as changing a car's motor oil and finding a new unfamiliar way to look at it is what makes cultural analysis valuable. This is carried out even further when combined with the process of the depth interview.

THE IN-DEPTH INTERVIEW

The in-depth interview[2] lies at the heart of ethnographic work and is most powerful for accessing the categories, assumptions, and logic by which the consumer makes decisions, views the world, and constructs patterns of daily experience. It provides understanding of the beliefs and experiences of the consumer and is crucial for gaining cultural knowledge on a subject. The interview can be understood as a social construction or production between the interviewer and the respondent. The interviewer and respondent work together to create meaning out of a conversation as both actively work to interpret what the other is after. As I discuss here, interviewing is inherently collaborative, and every interview is an interpersonal drama with a developing plot. The interviewer and respondent are participants in the process of meaning-making and storytelling, which is constructed in relation to the ongoing communicative contingencies of the interview process.

There are various approaches or types of interviewing styles that are useful in cultural analysis for anthropologists. *The active interview*, as discussed and elaborated by James Holstein and Jaber Gubrium (1995) is one of the most valuable and useful for anthropologists, specifically because it attends to empathy, it is collaborative with the respondent, and, most importantly, is co-created as a means to truly participate as a researcher.[3]

THE ACTIVE INTERVIEW METHOD

Our "interview society" dominates conversations on television, blogs, social media, and so forth. As a research method, interviewing is our main mode of systematic inquiry in the social sciences, marketing, advertising, media, politicians and pollsters. The challenge lies in gathering information that is reliable and meaningful. But cultural meaning on a topic is not simply existent in the respondent's head. It is constructed in the interview. This interactive style of interviewing is different in theory and practice from traditional interviewing.

As Holstein and Gubrium (1995, 8) detail, the traditional approach to interviewing sees the respondent as a "vessel of answers." Information that the subject possesses is viewed as passively contained, unchanging and uncontaminated in the head of the respondent. The focus of the interview is strictly on content, and the object for the source of information is the respondent. This simply requires the researcher to ask the right questions to extract or "pull information out." Unfortunately, this approach to interviews leads to a dry 'question and answer' format, analogous to a ping-pong effect of conducting a survey or questionnaire in formal interviews.

Instead, the active interview process of Holstein and Gubrium (1995) stresses an interactional style and approach to knowledge construction that is co-created between the interviewer and respondent. As discussed earlier, cultural analysis involves a process of co-creation and co-production with participants, a style that acknowledges interviewing people as an interpretive event, with respondents as active agents. Rather than excavating "facts" from a respondent's mind, the active interview involves meaning-making in the interview process. Respondents have their own authoritative voices in discerning and interpreting what is going on in their culture and in the interview setting. Information exchanged is actively interpreted and created between the two (or more) people present and occurs explicitly and implicitly. Participants are constantly developing new thoughts and measuring their responses as the interview proceeds. An interview as an active event can take any number of directions in its flow.

Different from the traditional interview format, active interviewing shouldn't just ask questions of the respondent, but attempt to incite *narrative production*. This moves the interview beyond simple, "yes"/"no" answers. The interviewer attempts to invoke stories on a topic from the respondent, followed by attention and involvement which works to guide the flow of the conversation. Interviews are, thus, actively observed as well as attended to as interactive events.

THE INTERVIEWER'S INFLUENCE ON THE SUBJECT

Interviews start with empathy, connecting with the respondent to build rapport. This might happen in sharing common background stories. Citing shared experience is a form of eliciting responses and helps frame the content of recalled experience, build a common framework, and share a level of rapport.

For instance, how the interviewer opens the line of questioning changes the flow of the whole interview. The opening not only initiates conversation, but it also frames the narrative and conditions the response of others. The respondent, meanwhile, is anticipating what the researcher wants to hear, so each introduction designates a distinctive perspective from which the person will respond. Using certain categories for opening tends to incite certain ways of thinking from the respondent and leads to assumptions and responses, while excluding others.

So, for example, informing the respondent that you are a researcher new to the US and are working as a "foreign student" in this country sets certain expectations. Expectations would change if you were to say, instead, that you are a "New Yorker," or identify as a "feminist" and ask what it's like for women to shop for new technology in a high-tech store. In this way, while you let the respondent become a storyteller, you are also conditioning responses from them.

When the interviewer suggests questions and prompts such as these, they act as framing devices (or themes for story codes). Codes, in this context, refers to an emic process that draws from language and the thinking of respondents. As the researcher enters conversation, he or she is assessing the embedded themes, concepts or metaphors that may arise in conversation, and what the person is referencing. Codes become a point of reference for the respondent which encourages the respondent to use examples that are comparable, while the researcher is listening for analogies, metaphors, and stories within stories. While interviewing skills include good listening skills, the researcher can also challenge responses, pose new thoughts, or suggest possibilities that the respondent hadn't considered. Stories elicited then can take any number of directions.

For another consideration, our memories are not fixed in our head, but are fluid. Thoughts that are recalled are continually reconsidered so that by framing questions with different probes or codes, new thoughts arise and ultimately shape answers. Amid conversations, when new considerations or themes arise, the respondent may explore new links between memories and experiences as the interviewer shapes questions. For example, the opening question, "Tell me about your life," can be reframed in terms of metaphors that elicit different types of experiences and memories, such as "what was your life *journey* about?" or "what were the major *turning points*?" or "what were the points in your life in which you *rebelled*?" Each line of questioning poses a different assumption of experience and may elicit different recollections from the respondent, whether recalling life as a journey, turning points, or moments of rebellion. The interviewer must be prepared for fluidity. Ethnographic guides are not scripts and improvisation during interviews can yield valuable findings and insights.

Finally, a salient skill of the active interviewer is the ability to detect what is not said through the shared sense of embodied presence with the informant. An astute anthropologist reads the context not only for positive information, such as what is said, done, and happening, but also for negative or absent information, or what is not said, done, or happening. Gillian Tett calls this skill "listening to social silence," to help us see what is in plain sight (2021, 139). Detecting and understanding subtle nuances in plain sight are largely enabled because of participating in "real time" in the co-presence of active social situations. When elements in a setting are not spoken about and are invisible, or perhaps even unspeakable, they affect any situation. In this case, silence can alert us to pay greater attention. Acoustic ecologists Hempton and Grossmann (2009, 2) claim,

> Silence is not the absence of something, but the presence of every-
> thing. Silence nurtures our human nature ... it leaves us with a more
> receptive mind and a more attuned ear, we become better listeners
> not only to nature but to each other.

Silence, they continue, calls upon a sense of presence. Jay Hasbrouck alerts us to be aware of this presence in "expanded awareness," in which we not only pay attention to what the informants tell us as a researcher, but what they neglect to tell us (2018, 16–21). Moments of silence, then, become opportunities, not hindrances, for our learning from interviews.

STORYTELLING AND CULTURAL ANALYSIS

When conducting an interview, Holstein and Gubrium (1995) alert us to two processes that need to be attended to: *how* the meaning-making process of the story unfolds is as crucial as knowing *what* is asked and conveyed to the respondent. This approach requires the participant observer to evoke probes at certain times and to listen carefully and observe throughout. First, attending to the "what" of the story focuses on the substance or *content* of what is said; listening to what something means to a person, and trying to understand why this is important. Simultaneously, attending to the "how" of the story focuses on observing the *process* of telling the story as it unfolds, attending to respondent body cues, emphatic rises in tone of voice, speeding up speaking at times of excitement, while at other times slowing down. The "how" of the story told explicates the ways in which the subject matter is organized and presented, and how it unfolds emotionally in the respondent's narrative construction.

In preparing for the interview, start with a general "grand tour" (Spradley 1979) or generalized questions that open the conversation. As you proceed in the interview, move from general to specific questions. Offer up topics to discuss and use probes to go deeper. Try to avoid yes or no responses. Moments of pause or silence in an interview are helpful and allow the respondent to contemplate a thought. Also, avoid asking "why" directly as a question, since, as Belk and colleagues (2013, 37) detail, asking people why "puts them on the defensive and makes them feel they need to justify and rationally explain their behavior, even though it was not rationally motivated." Instead, the researcher can ask "how come?" or, more specifically, "please elaborate." In addition, it may be useful to circle back to earlier topics or repeat back what the respondent says, for them to explain in more detail. Furthermore, in a good interview, listen for key words or phrases that stand out as significant. Don't answer for the respondent, but "playback" to them—let them finish or elaborate on a topic. This allows the respondent to develop a story further, letting them construct memories, items and events into a narrative, which leads to deeper meaning. Let's look at a transcript from an actual interview about a study on whole mouth health for a dental brand.

Anthropologist   We've talked a little bit about this. But let me ask you again. How does having nice teeth and a healthy mouth add to or take away from someone's overall appearance?

Respondent   I think having nice teeth definitely adds to your appearance. It makes you more attractive. Having a not-so-nice smile takes away from a person's beauty or appearance.

Anthropologist   Could you say... could you expand on that? ... you know, in what way ...?

Respondent   I had said before you can have the nicest outfit. You know, the nicest makeup, nicest hair and then your teeth are yellow or stained. That just ... It just takes away from the rest of you. Your mouth definitely stands out more than anything.

Anthropologist   OK, you're consistent here. Do you think it's more important for women to have beautiful teeth than for men, or is it equally important?

Respondent   No, equally important.

Anthropologist   And how so?

Respondent   I don't think of beauty just with women, you know, men too. I mean it's not called beauty, but handsomeness or whatever, right? Your having healthy teeth still reflects on that.

Anthropologist   What is it reflecting?

Respondent   The way a man would take care of himself, if he is ...you know, if he has yellow teeth or whatever, that's just not attractive. Or if a woman has yellow teeth, it's not attractive also.

Anthropologist   Let's take this even further. So ... You see somebody and they don't have great teeth and it says, "Well, they don't take very good care of their teeth." But then what do you think about them?

Respondent   And if they don't take very good care of their teeth, my guess is they probably don't have the best diet. They probably don't exercise. That's just what my impression would be. It may or may not be the case, but that's just what I get from someone whose teeth are not so great.

Anthropologist   OK. OK, so they don't have the best diet or exercise. And? ...

Respondent   They probably don't take care of themselves the way that they should.

Anthropologist   And? ...

Respondent   They just aren't healthy people in general.

Anthropologist   And? ....

(Respondent laughs demurely and pauses, reflecting)

Anthropologist   So, then what's your reaction to them? This person's clearly not taking good care of himself and so ... do you get a negative feel about that or ...?

Respondent   I guess as the first impression, yeah, I would probably have a negative. I would go with personality and stuff like that too, but, as a first impression, yeah, it probably means they are not a healthy person. You know, I'm trying to be a healthy person. If they're not, that's probably not someone who I would probably relate with ... or want to have a conversation with, I guess ... And that sounds snobby.

(She laughs again, turning away from the camera)

Anthropologist   You're taking this just to the kind of place I wanted. So, to be the person that you might not want to even be able to have a conversation with?

Respondent   Right. Sure, that I wouldn't be able to relate, I guess. And that's just based on my assumptions you know, I don't know. Maybe they are healthy, but that's just what I assume.

Anthropologist   And would that be because they seem to have different values from you, who are taking care of yourself and trying to eat right and exercise and all?

Respondent   I try. Yeah, that's right.

What do we make of this analysis? The anthropologist probes responses from the respondent, hoping to answer the "why" question to better understand mouth health, but without asking the respondent direct "why" questions. Nor does the anthropologist lead with yes and no questions, but rather use "probes" ("Is it more important for women than men to have beautiful teeth?"). She lets the respondent finish sentences, utilizing pauses for the respondent to think further, and repeats back and even challenges what the respondent last said for more clarification ("So, you might not want to even have a conversation with that person?"). Also, by "laddering up,"[4] the anthropologist prompts the respondent to elaborate further, interjecting "And ..." to encourage the respondent to further develop her narrative.

Making the familiar strange is what makes cultural analysis stand out. In this case, it's taking a familiar category, like brushing teeth, and finding a new way to look at it. Giovanni DaCol and David Graeber (2011, vii) hold that the making of the exotic is the domain of ethnography, because "... good ethnography makes everything exotic". Ethnography, they explain, is the pragmatic inquiry into events, revealing moments of speculative wonder that rearrange preconceived notions and categories by juxtaposing different cultural images and positions, often as an inversion of a relationship between familiar terms.

Here, the inversion the anthropologist found is something very culturally familiar: brushing teeth and having a clean white smile is not just a small part of health and beauty. Rather, as the respondent expressed, mouth health stands out as a key element of defining the whole person. All the anthropologist's skills are brought to bear in the interviewing process, encouraging the respondent to construct a story, which was co-created with the help of the anthropologist in the interview. This resulted in a rich description of a narrative in which we learned that whole mouth health is not just about a healthy mouth and nice smile, but indexical of the morals and character of the whole person.

ADDITIONAL TECHNIQUES TO AID ETHNOGRAPHIC RESEARCH

Other techniques can be used to supplement ethnographic research and assist the researcher in a project. *Focus groups* are more widely used in consumer or user experience research for business than in academic research. As Sunderland and Denny (2007) maintain, focus groups reflect an "ethnography of speaking" where talk by participants is socially and collectively performative. The moderator can focus on what respondents say, or the "what" of the conversation, and on the "how" information is told, as a means for understanding the research issues in question. This approach is similar to the discussion in *The Active Interview* and to the collective construction of meaning that is produced by the group. In a well-conducted focus group, the moderator can nurture a creative environment and a free-form sharing of opinions that produces a collectively created discussion on a topic.

Projective methods are also useful to help respondents articulate what they may have difficulty in explaining in words. As detailed in Belk et al. (2013) *word associations* give respondents a series of words and require them to respond back with the first idea that comes to mind. If the word "beer" is suggested, the respondent might respond with "sloppy"—which provides an unguarded, unfiltered top-of-mind association that may be useful. *Sentence completion* is a similar exercise intended to produce unfiltered top-of-mind associations (i.e., "Christmas is a time when …"). Filling out *diaries*, either online or with portable notebooks, allows respondents to extend thoughts either before or after the ethnographic interview. This is a great way to draw out further information over an extended time and in different contexts.

Filling in *thought bubbles* that are associated with a drawing or picture is also a helpful tool to have respondents explain what is going on. *Object personification*—"If this brand were a social media celebrity, who would it be?—could be asked as a question or by asking a respondent to bring a picture out of a magazine or from the web and create a story that expresses how the image exemplifies the personified object.

Another useful tool which could be employed is having respondents create a *collage* that expresses a theme of interest—such as putting on make-up in the morning. We used this for the Revlon research (discussed in Chapter 3) which expressed in imagery the thoughts and feelings about wearing make-up and the transformation in self that occurs before and after applying cosmetics. These images narrate a story that the respondent may not fully express in words, and, as in other interviews, the journey of revelation reveals a process of making invisible culture more discerning and visible to researchers.

***

PART II: OVERVIEW OF VARIOUS RESEARCH METHODOLOGIES: WHEN TO APPLY WHICH METHOD

Even though cultural analysis offers distinct advantages to conducting research, not all research questions are answered by ethnography. Different kinds of research and their methodologies produce different kinds of "truth." Not only are there multiple types of qualitative and quantitative research methods, but they can also be combined in multiple ways (cf. Ladner 2019). The approaches we take as researchers shape the way we conduct research, the theories we use to interpret our findings, and, importantly, the outcomes of our findings we might expect to produce.

For instance, work in UX research is often heuristic; that is, best fit and adaptive, which means using the best tool at hand for the business and research question. On occasion, research questions are best answered with a rapidly distributed survey, or, at other times, qualitative research in the form of an ethnographic study could be preferred, such as when conducting exploratory research into why consumers do the things they do. Often, research requires some form of quantified validation that can help determine what causes something else to happen, and, in such a case, quantitative analysis is called for. On still other occasions, the use of a mix-method design, which integrates qualitative and quantitative, multiple forms of qualitative, or multiple forms of quantitative, can be used to make the study more comprehensive or complete than if a single method is used.

The important issue to remember is that research needs are not alike. Research provides tools, as in qualitative, quantitative and mixed-method approaches, that can address the client's research question differently, while all methods help to develop the results into a powerful and compelling story about their consumer.

RESEARCH NEEDS TO TELL A STORY

As human beings, our most important form of communication is through narration. We think and tell other people things about ourselves through the stories we tell. As researchers in anthropology, our most powerful stories are the ones we tell about the consumers, or product users, or employees in a company that we investigate. Anthropologist Paul Stoller (2007) claims that telling stories speaks to the most human of things: fear, pain, love, fate, and humor; it is our scholarly obligation to tell stories. Hasbrouck (2018, 89) adds that stories not only introduce ideas, images, and facts that resonate on many levels for listeners, they integrate elements of logic, reason, or rationality along with imagery, emotion, and personal experiences, into a compelling whole. Archaeologists unearth vast stories in hieroglyphics on the great pyramids of Giza, Egypt; along the cave walls of Altamira in Northern Spain; among the Mayan manuscripts in the Yucatan peninsula of Central America, to name just a few important sites. Stories are what make us human, they help teach us, put facts into a compelling and memorable form, and stories in our research help clients understand and remember their consumers better.

Telling a story out of data from our research can involve qualitative or quantitative methods, or both as mixed methods. Ladner explains (2019) when we let our research tell a story, we are explaining our data in a way that presents dynamic characters in action, follows a plotline, and is structured with a resolve or conclusion. This pattern is recognized by us, so facts become more memorable when situated in a narrative context. Whatever the case, our goal as researchers is to use methods that can help us organize the data so they can answer the research question in an interesting way.

WHICH TO USE: QUALITATIVE, QUANTITATIVE, OR MIXED METHODS?

Qualitative and quantitative research approaches draw from different philosophical traditions and tell different stories about our research. Deductive research starts from a set of general premises, formulating a hypothesis before research begins, then setting out the appropriate steps in an investigation by narrowing variables in the research design and drawing out a specific conclusion within the parameters of the experiment itself. Inductive research involves an opposite trajectory, starting with contextual data and forming general theories from specific observations that arise in the context being researched. Anthropologists practice inductive research in ethnography, observing and interviewing people in a contextual setting, where they note the occurrence of something repeatedly, leading them to identify a pattern, and from identifying a pattern, arriving at some theoretical or generalizable understanding.

How we first collect the data starts with the types of questions we wish to answer and will proceed in what type of research approach we should take. Differences between quantitative and qualitative approaches to consumer, brand, design, and organizational research have different purposes, lead to different outcomes, and form different stories, because of the ways they approach problems and the types of answers they seek.

Starting with the type of question your research hopes to address: are you seeking *depth of meaning* to illuminate something, or do you wish to *validate and confirm* something that already exists? Addressing these questions requires different research approaches. For instance, do you wish to better understand the experience of a particular brand in a consumer's life, or you wish to better understand the values, motivations, and behaviors of a community of employees in your company, or learn what are the untapped needs and drivers of consumers in a brand category? These types of questions suggest a *qualitative research approach*.

In other cases, the research question might be seeking to validate some earlier findings, so that you might be able to predict in future events a sample size for a larger generalized population. Questions of validation might measure how many people noticed your client's brand in advertising messages, or how often these messages were noticed. This is important when testing various media, such as ads on social media, out-of-home ads as on billboards, in newsprint, and so forth. Do you wish to measure responses to see if the brand communication is relevant? Or do you wish to ascertain if people changed their opinions about the brand because of seeing your ad? For answering these questions of *causation* or to measure the *scale of an effect*, quantitative research is best suited to provide the answers.

When investigating complex phenomena with multiple levels of measurement, such as the individual consumer experience of a brand *and* the larger behavioral response across multiple markets, or if the researcher wants to explore a question at the macro level (the collective ethos of a corporate campaign on its mission statement or shared values) as well as at the micro level (how well it resonates with individual employees), then mixed-methods design is best applied. Two qualitative approaches can combine in a singular study to provide an inductive theoretical thrust with complementary angles to explore an issue, as exemplified in the following case.

Robert Morais (2020), a business anthropologist, applied a mixed methods approach that combined psychological with anthropological projects to elucidate the deeper meaning of pet food in American culture. The case study illustrates how two qualitative approaches were used to generate brand positioning ideas for a popular pet food brand.

Freshpet dog food is made of high-quality ingredients that mirror homemade food owners might serve their dogs. One of the business challenges was its unusual location in the refrigerated section of stores, since customers unfamiliar with the brand tended to walk right past it. Cultural familiarity with the dog food category normally locates canned or bagged food in the pet food aisle of the store and not in a refrigerator. Research questions and objectives, centered around how to disrupt "autopilot" buying habits of potential prospects who do not buy Freshpet and to discover new ways to deepen the relationship with current Freshpet users.

First, focus group research delved into psychological dimensions of pet ownership with respondents. Interviewing techniques such as *guided retrospection* that probed the emotions respondents associated with feeding their pets, and *deprivation scenarios* (what respondents would feed their dog in the absence of Freshpet), revealed how dogs are treated as members of the family.

In a separate but related study, in-store ethnographies revealed ways to make the brand's unusual refrigerator location, which was sometimes bypassed by dog food shoppers, more "category familiar." Morais recommended that the company work with designers to increase the "stopping power" of Freshpet's refrigerated case in or near the pet food aisle.

His final insight stemmed from what was earlier referred to in this chapter as a process of constructing, co-creating, and producing a finding. Based on a cognitive classification interviewing process in people's homes, Morais proposed to the client that Freshpet be positioned above dry and wet food and below the gold standard of home cooked human food. Adapting Maslow's phrase, "Hierarchy of Needs", Morais labeled the positioning "The Hierarchy of Feed," an approach that would situate the brand in consumers' minds more closely to human food than dry or wet dog food and offer a way for dog owers to enhance their pet's eating experience and express their love for their dog. Using a mixed methods approach of psychology in focus groups and anthropological ethnography applied to market research added value because it brought methodological and theoretical breadth to the research questions and sparked insights that singularly designed studies might not.

QUANTITATIVE RESEARCH AND THE STORIES THEY TELL

The quantitative researcher might start a project by using concepts and measures important to the company, using a sharp lens to bring a narrow strip of study into precise focus. The goal of the research is to isolate and define analytic categories as precisely as possible before a study begins. Then, once the study is undertaken, make no further changes to determine the relationship between them. Closed questions with fixed responses are sought when questions allow the respondent to respond directly, unambiguously, and in large volume. So, for instance, if investigating a restaurant chain, the researcher may use variables in a survey that inquire how many people frequent a place, what times are busiest, which menu items are most popular, how many staff work there, how much money is earned. This type of research and data collection can be applied to smaller samples and then generalized to a larger population. It also does not require the presence of the researcher, so data can be compared across different locations without ever having to visit them. This is ideal for cross-sectional research of large populations and various locations.

In using quantitative research to tell a story, the characters are not individual actors, since you are often working with large data sets. Rather, social categories or identified themes that arise in the data tell the story. A complex social category such as "gender" or "race" can be shown to be nuanced and is not simplistic. For instance, Sam Ladner (2019), 71–72) provides a description of a deductive study she sets up, which begins with a clear hypothesis that she as a researcher wishes to prove or disprove. Her hypothesis to test for the company is: "Women employees are more satisfied than men employees." Background information on employee satisfaction from a previous survey demonstrates in her study that women in the company are more satisfied than men. The researcher is then testing this premise and may have reason to believe it is still true. So, the researcher then sets out to prove/disprove this assertion. The researcher collects data that asks about gender and satisfaction and runs a test of significance to see if the responses from men and women differ in a reliable way. As it turns out in the research, Ladner finds that women are more likely to agree with the statement, "It is satisfying working at this company." In this way, deductive reasoning and quantitative research measure the pervasiveness of the thing already known, "employee satisfaction," which the new research sets out to confirm or disprove.

The advantage of quantitative research is that it sets a benchmark for a time and a situation, such as in the consumer marketplace, or an internal company population, which then can be tested repeatedly. In this case, it tests against possible new variables, such as implementing new company policies that need to be validated against employee work satisfaction. Ladner's story of employee satisfaction would be beneficial to affirm if it was positive, or, if negative, to help modify company policies and improve work-force culture.

QUALITATIVE RESEARCH AND THE STORIES THEY TELL

In qualitative research, stories are essential, especially if ethnographic research is used to report findings or insights gained from cultural understanding. Stories then become enmeshed in the core of cultural analysis itself. The following story, based upon my ethnographic research conducted among Cadillac's target buyers, reveals how cultural analysis uncovered a hidden narrative of pursuing the "American Dream". That storyline led to repositioning the brand as earned success.

Cadillac was once the premiere luxury automobile in the US. But hurt by increased competition, lackluster products, and an aging buyer base, in 2000 Cadillac ranked in sixth place in the luxury car market, behind Lexus, Mercedes Benz, BMW, Acura, and Audi. Moreover, Cadillac was not deemed relevant to the lives of the company's desired 30–50-year-old targets. I was working at D'Arcy Masius Benton and Bowles, the advertising agency for Cadillac, and our Account Planning team was presented with a challenge to reposition the iconic brand.

Cadillac redesigned its product line in 2002 but needed a major consumer insight to formulate a new strategy and positioning. Quantitative surveys told us that Cadillac had an "old problem": it did not address what many people wanted in a luxury car. Respondents in focus groups characterized Cadillac as a "floaty boat" for "blue-haired old ladies in Boca Raton Florida," and a brand that just was not "cool."

In our ethnographic research, instead of asking prospective Cadillac buyers what they wanted in a luxury car, we asked a different set of questions about cultural meaning. We asked what success meant, what it means to "make it" in America, and what are the "markers" of success?

We learned that potential Cadillac buyers, especially those new to wealth, felt that after hard work, they wanted their success to be celebrated. "You celebrate when you finally arrive!" We learned that their stories of success were essential to their identity and to fulfilling the "American Dream." Respondents believed that through all their work, imagination, and innovation, they were accomplishing the extraordinary and they wanted to show it off; they had a desire to feel—and be seen as—above and beyond the ordinary.

Based upon this cultural understanding about success in America, we positioned Cadillac as the fulfillment of the American Dream. We then cast it in a commercial as a powerful story of self-reinvention. The story of "breaking through" barriers and earning success was relevant, not to foreign cars or their owners, but to Americans who had finally arrived. Cadillac was their celebration of success.

The Cadillac "breakthrough" advertising campaign was launched featuring Led Zeppelin's music during the 2002 Super Bowl. It was a call to action from General Motors, Cadillac's parent company (its comeback), and for successful people, as an expression of self-reinvention. The campaign ran from 2002 to 2005, advancing Cadillac from sixth to third place in the luxury car market, and, as a percentage, Cadillac outsold all other GM lines. The tagline, "For those who have arrived" is still used in Cadillac advertising today.

CONCLUSION

The aim of this chapter is to lead students and practitioners of business anthropology to better understand the value of anthropological thinking and uses of cultural analysis in uncovering latent meanings that often remain invisible in other forms of research. Research methods used in ethnography and blended with other quantitative methods or other qualitative forms offer clients robust approaches to answering a range of research questions. Cultural analysis aided by other forms of consumer research thus can provide solutions and offer relevant client recommendations that make sense of complexity by identifying the underlying meaning behind human behaviors, even as culture is always changing and evolving.

As this chapter has also shown, cultural analysis used by anthropologists often involves collaborative teamwork with others in various disciplines as well as with colleagues of anthropologists working in multisite locations. Anthropologists, therefore, have an opportunity to increase their impact in society and raise public awareness of their work and make anthropology relevant to broader audiences.

NOTES

1 See Sunderland and Denny (2003), and Morais and Malefyt (2010).
2 See Belk et al. (2013) and Grant McCracken (1988).
3 Also, James P. Spradley (1979).
4 Laddering represents the linkage in thoughts between a basic explanation and higher order perceptual process of consumers. See Reynolds and Cutman (1988).

3

ANTHROPOLOGY IN CONSUMER RESEARCH

Anthropologists working in or for business frequently conduct consumer research for their corporate clients in fields of marketing and advertising, product development, market research, UX research, social media, sustainable consumption and cross-cultural consumer research. Their primary focus in research is to discover the manifest and hidden cultural meaning of products, brands, and services in the everyday lives of people, and report this information back to their corporate clients. They also inform their clients of the varied social practices of consumers (such as cooking, cleaning, driving a car, online activity) in which the clients' products, brands, and services are used for specific purposes and become meaningful. In this way, anthropologists use the results from consumer research to help organizations solve business problems and develop creative strategies and processes to deliver improvements to their brands, products, and services for consumers.

Beyond representing the cultural meaning of products, brands, and services in research, anthropologists also interpret consumer discourses and observe patterns of behavior in cultural analysis that show human agency in creative and often unexpected ways. Bringing to light the unexpected uses of things in cultural practice frequently leads to new considerations or even innovations in products or services under investigation. Anthropology in consumer research can, thus, help to reveal the hidden domains of consumers' cultural practices that often lead to creative outcomes. This can help organizations to deliver innovative new products and services to customers that they previously had not considered. In fields of organizational management and market research, innovation is considered key to commercial success.

DOI: 10.4324/9781003358930-3

In fleshing out discoveries, the larger role for business anthropologists is to act as mediators or facilitators between the world of consumers and corporations. As facilitators, anthropologists not only bring to light the taken for granted domains of cultural experience but also, by applying new considerations to existing or new products and services, anthropologists can initiate positive change between producers and consumers. When anthropological theory interprets consumer discourse and practices in consumer research, it can help determine a new significance for marketplace findings and make meaningful and impactful recommendations that are actionable for the client, and, at times, better for the world.

In this chapter, I discuss consumer research in these areas as a process of discovery of the taken for granted or invisible dimensions of culture which become evident not only by being there in context with the consumer, but by partaking in their actions. Knowing and learning is a process of *going along*, writes anthropologist, Tim Ingold. What is natural, tacit or invisible about cultural practices, becomes evident *in the doing*, where "knowing is movement" (2013, 1) and, reciprocally, movement is knowing. When consumer research is anthropological in its approach, it is about "knowing from the inside" (ibid.) and makes it distinct from other external-oriented approaches. Being "in" the experiences of others, not afar or outside of it, as put forward in surveys or artificial settings of focus groups, lets researchers *grow into knowledge* from corresponding *with* researchers, clients, and consumers themselves. In the cultural analysis of consumer contexts, this not only reveals unexpected insights for clients, but can also create positive outcomes in products and services, as indicated in the following study conducted for the Campbell's soup company.

CREATING POSITIVE CHANGE IN EVERYDAY MEALS

The Campbell's soup company, one of BBDO advertising's clients at the time, enlisted the help of my group, Cultural Discoveries, to explore the ways in which mothers (their target) came up with meal ideas for their families. The client had positioned the key research objective as understanding the cooking challenges and pressures mothers faced daily when confronting the 6:00 p.m. "dinner dilemma": what to make for dinner. Our project was ethnographic in nature, conducting 48 in-home interviews with middle-class women in their twenties to mid-sixties, most of whom were mothers of children living at home, in four US cities (see McCabe and Malefyt 2013).

As anthropologists, we wanted to understand the underlying social factors and cultural practices that women (and men) encounter when preparing the daily family meal. Part of the research was to investigate how US women think about meal preparation and construct dinner plans daily. In-home conversations with women, tours of their kitchens, and observation of women cooking a meal for the family, plus a brief food shopping excursion to observe how they thought about meals, rounded out the project parameters. Participants also kept journals of their daily thoughts and feelings around meal planning over the course of a week prior to the interview, and made collages of their favorite meals, adding a fuller ethnographic account of their behaviors. Nevertheless, observation of women cooking a family meal revealed a previously unknown insight on how improvisation implicitly guides and structures many women's cooking practices, even when following planned out recipes.

The women we spoke to had previously discussed with us the repertoire of favorite meals their families enjoyed and also that they occasionally experimented with new dishes. Yet, even as mothers cooked and talked with us about their actions while cooking, we noted how they altered ingredients as they moved along, adding less of this, more of that, substituting one ingredient for another, based on their knowledge of personal preferences for each member of the household. Changes, such as substituting cinnamon for cumin, demonstrated creative adaptations to recipes that were not articulated in prior discussions. Improvisation, as it were, became apparent in the expressions of embodied actions (visceral, felt, or enlivened bodily experiences) as care in action. As sociologist Richard Sennett (2008, 177, 189) describes in *The Craftsman*, thinking and feeling are contained within the process of making something. Embodied cooking practices allow the cook to develop specific skills and rituals, developing a sense of anticipation for the outcome, which often goes unspoken. "Gastronomy is a narrative", he claims, in which the cook "moves *through* the narrative," and "by imagining the whole process, you get outside yourself."

The tacit satisfaction of anticipating and imagining the whole family eating together had inspired the improvisational moves we observed from these women in preparing the daily meal.

Women's cooking practices of improvisation often go unnoticed and remain invisible, since many cultural practices lie hidden as being taken for granted. In this case, it was only during the process of observing and conversing with women *while they cooked*, while being "in" their experience of cooking, that the insight became apparent, and not in previous conversations Observing women improvise to satisfy the tastes of everyone in the family revealed that preparing dinners was a tacit way of recreating family life. Creativity in everyday life begins with making small adjustments with the familiar, rather than making a complete departure from something new and non-existent. Tweaking family favorites was a positive message we shared with Campbell's, rather than framing cooking in the negative as a "dinner dilemma."

Moreover, facilitating a positive outcome for the study later on, back at the agency, was furthered by our learning about the social ways women gathered meal ideas from other women, whether meeting friends for lunch, watching Rachael Ray on television, discussing meals with work colleagues, or emailing suggestions to friends. This networked resource of familiar people that women draw from daily contrasted with the structured and authoritative stance towards meals on the company's website. Campbell's had promoted many of its popular cooking recipes on the web as designed and recommended by their notable chefs. We advised the company to modify their website by implementing a star rating system that featured suggestions and improvements from *women users themselves* who cooked the recipes and made adjustments to them, not the chefs. This change, we explained, mirrored women's own natural approach to gathering ideas from friends, so that recipes on the website were imparted from the "ground up," not "top down." Such consumer research produced positive results for meal creation by drawing on the collaborative efforts of consumers.

The most useful, informative, and "disruptive" (to use a marketing term) forms of consumer research are developed from ideas that are produced "in" contexts with others during their activity, which makes all research *collaborative*. Insights are collaboratively produced not only by working with consumers, but also with other researchers, designers, scholar practitioners, ad creatives, clients, and so forth. Any "discovery" is a co-created process of construction and negotiation between interviewer, respondent, and the "situated context," whether online or off, or with others, at every stage of the research and development process. Consumer research and the shared ideas that are co-created with others also help corporations develop better products and improve existing services, because they more accurately represent the natural domain of cultural experience from whence they were created. Consumer research produced in this way can ethically instigate positive change in the corporate world and beyond, as will be discussed in this chapter.

THEORETICAL VIEWS IN CONSUMER RESEARCH

An ongoing challenge to the popularity of ethnography in consumer research has been the gradual "decoupling" of ethnographic methods from anthropological theory, as ethnography is used in other forms of non-anthropological consumer research. The practice of ethnography has been incorporated or "hybridized" into other disciplines and professions where ethnography has now become "a business service" (Baba 2014, 56). Many research firms offer various forms of ethnography, including technology enhanced methods or "techno-methodologies" (Malefyt 2009). Cell phone calls, digital photo-reporting, blogging, and other technologies collect a rapid response from those studied, recording respondents in any context, and conducted by anyone who can wield the equipment, including the consumers themselves. However, mostly absent in these forms of data gathering is any form of anthropological analysis.

In contrast, consumer research using cultural analysis is guided by anthropological and other humanistic theories. Much of the theoretical tradition that guides anthropologists conducting consumer research draws from studies in symbolic, interpretive, and linguistic anthropology. These theoretical ways of thinking build on the idea that cultural analysis involves a philosophical tradition and a way of knowing (epistemology) people and their cultural processes in the contexts in which they happen. Meanings, artifacts and environments in which people live and relate to others are socially constructed through practices and discourses (ways of speaking) and are symbolically rich but also largely go unnoticed. In these contexts, anthropologists attempt to discern and clarify the associated socio-cultural practices that bring meaning to human life. The relevance of knowing cultural theories and traditional studies on topics like ritual, gift exchange, or gender dynamics, for example, is that if students are familiar with such theories, they can more easily recognize their expression when they encounter them among human actors in cultural contexts.

A useful anthropological theorist whose work is often applied to cultural analysis is Clifford Geertz (2000). His analysis of interpretive anthropology and understanding the "webs of significance" of culture in ethnography, as discussed earlier, are ways of understanding behavior in a social context and making the invisible of culture visible. The interpretive researcher goes beyond merely describing things and attempts to explain the meanings that people collectively ascribe to material objects, people, and events in their lives and in the world. This process involves cultural analysis, not just recording and playing back what people do or say in other contexts.

Victor Turner is another popular theoretical figure who anchored his symbolic investigations of African cultural life in social processes, which is evident in his work on rituals and rites of passage that includes social phenomena such as communitas (group togetherness), liminality, and other vital concepts useful in consumer research. Cultural analysis in consumer research seeks to identify the symbolic meaning of these social processes in consumption, consumer agency, and the cultural meaning of consumer practices in everyday patterns. For instance, Turner's theoretical concept of liminality as detailed in *The Ritual Process* (1969) is helpful in explaining "in-between" cultural objects and practices in everyday life.

Theoretically, liminality, or "threshold," is a transitional stage of ambiguity that occurs in the middle stage of a rite of passage, when participants "stand between" their previous identity, time, or community, and a new way. College students, for instance, are in a liminal period—no longer children but not quite socially integrated as working adults. While liminality represents a transitory period of change, uncertainty, and ambiguity in moving from one stage to another, it also encompasses a fluid state of malleable opportunity for new structures and/or customs to become established. Liminal qualities can also be ascribed to material objects and can be used as a point at which to recognize consumer innovation in product development.

The concept of liminality as an unfinished and malleable quality of something in transition became evident in a research project involving packaging ideas for a consumer food product. Liminality helped to explain consumer behavior and make visible cultural processes of innovation in food preparation.

SPAM AS A LIMINAL FOOD

In a study for the processed meat product, Spam, my team at BBDO set out to explore the brand in people's lifestyles, attitudes, and behavior. The client, Hormel foods, wished to consider packaging options for Spam beyond selling it as a slab of meat in a can. Package ideas such as single slices for sandwiches, a diced pack for salads, or other options were considered. Research into consumer meal preparation with new packaging ideas would allow BBDO to develop a range of fresh communication opportunities for Spam.

We conducted ten ethnographic interviews with couples and families from African American, Latino, and White backgrounds, and hosted four group parties with Spam lovers in three consumer markets of Los Angeles, California, San Antonio, Texas and Charlotte, North Carolina. Our in-home visits included watching respondents prepare a meal in the kitchen with Spam, shop for food items at the grocery store, as well as a photo assignment and product sort of images to ascertain cultural categories of various food groups and expand the ethnographic collection of data.

Previous consumer surveys conducted by Hormel stressed the convenience of new packaging ideas. However, being up close, in-person with consumers, cooking in their kitchens, revealed an unspoken quality of Spam that inspires creativity from individuals. We learned that Spam is a versatile product that can be eaten for any meal, any time, almost anywhere. Spam lovers described how the product can stand out as a meat centerpiece or be disguised and blend into recipes as an ingredient. But Spam goes beyond functionality to inspire creative individuality.

In our ethnography, we witnessed a multitude of ways the unformed slab out of the can is creatively turned into something appetizing and delicious. We watched inspiration in action as cooks shredded, diced, sliced or "spiraled" Spam into various familiar recipes or created new recipes. One respondent said, "I try different recipes, all different kinds ... sometimes I create them in my mind. I think, what would be good together [with Spam]?" "You get creative with it, add it into an omelet, make a sandwich, use it in a casserole." Another respondent said, "You can manipulate it into things, because it is so versatile." Creativity begins as a journey of transforming a staple, taking a shapeless, liminal slab and making it into something new and appealing.

In our final report to Hormel, we stated that although the product is fully cooked, Spam is not finished. It's a liminal object that gives agency to cooks, who creatively transform it into whatever they desire. We positioned it as an "idea catalyst" for meals. We recommended against the new packaging ideas since selling it in pre-formed slices or diced in pre-packaged containers would *remove* the creative agency from the cook in reconfiguring Spam to their liking. Instead, we suggested taking the notion of "idea catalyst" for the brand and launching a cooking competition on Facebook, challenging other Spam enthusiasts in cook-offs at local fairs around the country. They agreed. The winners at fairs won prizes and posted their recipes on Facebook in a successful marketing campaign for the brand.

As for other theories in action, from a linguistic standpoint, George Lakoff and Mark Johnson's *Metaphors We Live By* (2003) provides a theory of how everyday metaphors orient our thinking and behavior and has been highly useful in consumer research. Metaphors have been harnessed for decades by various corporate firms to guide a company's mission, to shape its storytelling, and create an internal culture. Metaphors also communicate the brand ideal (its ultimate aspirational expression) to consumers, so metaphors are frequently used in advertising.

For instance, Southwest Airlines sought to change the airline industry by focusing on a friendlier customer experience. In 1977 it adopted the ticker symbol LUV, and since then, the heart has become the carrier's main visual symbol of this commitment to service. Love is a metaphorical device in their mission statement and their service commitment: they have served "LUV bites" as snacks on planes and dispensed tickets from "LUV machines." Much of Southwest's marketing and internal material is based on the concept of spreading love and care. Anthropologist Ken Erickson works with airlines such as JAL, Boeing, and others, and helps them craft such stories to improve customer experience as he develops brand and marketing ideas through symbolic analysis and the use of language in culture.

Briefly, other theories used in consumer research include power relations, embodiment and perception through the body, the senses, emotion, relationship of persons with material things; gender, law, entrepreneurship; creativity; money and economics; globalization; cultural change; kinship and networks or assemblages of people, things, practices, institutions, and discourses; magic; totemism and gift exchange.

Marcel Mauss's theory of gift exchange (2000) has been used to explain gift giving processes, such as expressing differences in gender relations. Russell Belk (2020) has shown that there are numerous everyday gifts that help stitch together the fabric of friendships and hold them together. Theoretical understanding of exchanges can explain gender differences in gift giving. He explains that Mauss's theory of the gift is used to create social bonds, in that, beyond market transactions that are functional and complete with no social ties, the gift, as Mauss details, creates bonds of reciprocity with the obligation to reciprocate. In gender terms, while some men tend to view the world in terms of commodity exchanges, in which there are no lingering feelings of indebtedness or interpersonal bonds, some women see the world in terms of social exchanges, which create ongoing linkages, bonds, and gratitude. Belk used these ideas in a study of the gift giving dynamics of lipstick.

INNOVATION AND CONSUMER RESEARCH

Consumer anthropologists have also worked with companies on product development innovations. Ethnography can reveal how a product performs and is valued by customers in usage situations. It can motivate product improvements and spark questions for testing in subsequent quantitative studies. The case of WD-40 illustrates the use of ethnography as part of a multiphase marketing research project.

WD-40 is a canned lubricant and rust preventive that, for decades, was sold with an attachable plastic straw that enabled users to apply it with precision. In the early 2000s, the WD-40 company was confronted with inroads from competitive brands and was considering product innovations. The R&D group designed a mechanical applicator that was permanently built into the WD-40 sprayer. That innovation, which the company called "Smart Straw," solved a common user problem: losing the straw. Despite the promise of Smart Straw, company management was reluctant to change the WD-40 can, out of fear that a modification might alienate long-time users. An ethnographic project was a game-changer. Researchers watched as a printing technician used a brand competitive to WD-40. When consumer anthropologist Robert Morais asked why he chose that brand over WD-40, he said he did not want to take time to walk across the room for WD-40. His response was a shock to the WD-40 marketing team; WD-40 was not worth taking ten steps. That finding led to additional qualitative research and motivated WD-40 management to field a quantitative test of base WD-40 versus WD-40 Smart Straw to assess the viability of replacing the base product with Smart Straw. Following that study, WD-40 Smart Straw was launched and was a major marketplace success.

Innovation is, thus, made apparent in cultural analysis from learning *with* consumers, being "in" their activities. Innovative ways to modify Spam came out of watching their practices for meal ideas. In other cases, innovation in consumer research came from the anthropologist's observations of embodied tacit experiences, such as noticing the workshop employee who didn't wish to be interrupted in the flow or rhythm of his work. Not only did Morais learn about issues regarding the value or worth of WD40 to the respondent (not deemed important enough to walk across the room to retrieve it), but this insight would not have been learned in focus groups, surveys or other non-contextual data gathering methods. Anthropological analysis requires being "in" the flow of the context, *with* the consumer, to know the process *from the inside*.

USER EXPERIENCE STUDIES

UX research has become one of the fastest-growing markets for anthropologists in consumer research. UX involves studying and understanding the perceptions, behaviors, and needs of users when interacting with a product or service, to enhance the design and usability of products or services. UX research is invaluable for creating successful digital products and services, such as software.

Using various research methods such as interviews, testing, and field studies, UX researchers gain valuable insights into user behavior that inform the design process. While UX researchers come from many fields, including human–computer interaction (HCI), design, and psychology, anthropologists bring special skills to the field. Skills such as empathy, an understanding of context, cultural relativism, and systems-thinking, as well as qualitative methodologies and skills in synthesizing data and storytelling provide an advantage for anthropologists. UX researchers also require skills in business training, research operations, and skills in quantitative methodologies, such as developing surveys and questionnaires, usability testing and design, eye-tracking, user analytics, and other quantitative research methods. By applying various consumer research methods, UX professionals can gain valuable insights into users' needs, preferences, and pain points. This information helps inform design decisions and create more user-centered experiences.

THE ULTIMATE UBER RIDE

In one example of studying UX, Uber sought to make carpooling more affordable and reliable for riders, and more effortless for its drivers. In 2014, the company test-launched uberPOOL to make it easy for riders to share their trip with other riders heading in the same direction. The mechanics of uberPOOL is the intelligence that matches riders for a trip, which can introduce various uncertainties into the user experience. Core to the business objective is understanding how to deliver a "Perfect POOL" experience—an ideal situation when three people in the vehicle get in and out at the same time and same location, allowing for a more predictable and affordable experience.

UX research conducted by Jenny Lo and Steve Morseman (2018) discovered that, for a reduced fare and a more direct route, riders were willing to forego the convenience of getting picked up at their door, in exchange for waiting and walking a certain distance to meet their Uber driver.

Their research design combined qualitative and quantitative studies to understand these user trade-offs to maximize the user's experience. The researchers used a mix of in-person interviews and two large-scale surveys, each with a different purpose. The investigation started with a multi-city qualitative research study designed to understand how users make trade-offs among their transportation options, suggesting key characteristics of a "Perfect POOL." The team followed up with a survey to validate these characteristics and identify the factors most important for riders' decisions. The team subsequently explored ways to translate the trade-offs back into the product experience. Learnings from their multi-phase research led to the successful Beta-launch of Express POOL in November 2017.

IMPROVING THE ZILLOW EXPERIENCE

In another example, Zillow, the real estate company, was undergoing a major change in transitioning from a digital marketplace for real estate advertising into a broad platform to support a variety of customer services, including buying, selling, and renting homes. To expand their services, the company needed to understand existing and potential users, and their experiences as they interact with Zillow's products and services.

Researchers Rebecca Hazen and colleagues (2020), set out with an Experience Measurement Program that provided feedback on how well Zillow experiences met users' needs and expectations as they progress through their real estate exploration journey. The process the researchers created and implemented mapped out an experience journey to capture and objectively assess the quality of user experiences as they occurred across digital, physical, and human-based touchpoints. The researchers identified what was important and made for a good experience, as well as defining metrics and developing measurement plans to reflect the nature of these experiences.

The Experience Measurement Program Framework first gathered contextual information from users. When interviewing respondents (renters) who were seeking to find homes, to access the hidden cultural meanings of home ownership, the researchers asked what makes for a good experience. Researchers also asked participants to talk through similar questions and walk through a journey for a similar activity in an entirely different domain, such as what they did to seek out a favorite restaurant. This type of questioning helped bring to the surface elements that people value, but do not fully realize or readily verbalize for the real estate market. This helped researchers apply what they learned in concepts to the rental scenario, then reconcile their findings for an overall improved service experience for customers.

RESEARCHING CONSUMER RESISTANCE TO CONSUMPTION

Consumer research in anthropology isn't always directed for the immediate benefit of corporations. Anthropologists also research emergent and rising consumer movements that signal signs of resistance or alternative forms of consumption in society. Growing aversion to consumption is evident in "emancipatory" social movements, which explore the ways consumers resist rampant consumerism or find creative ways to adapt and change consumption. This information is important to companies that seek alternative ways to develop sustainable products and services that appeal to "green" customers.

Consumers looking for different consumption practices find them in a variety of settings, including refurbished festival malls (European-style, often open-air, shopping markets that aim to revitalize downtown areas in major US cities), flea markets, and shopping at second-hand thrift stores. These sites respond to environmental concerns of waste, but also to nostalgic ideals of consumers, as people adopt more of an aesthetic ethos that seeks artwork, craft activities, and hand-crafted designer goods, not available in mass-market shopping settings. Other alternative forms of consumption, such as the slow food movement and return of local farmers' markets indicate that consumers are increasingly aware of the dangers of mass-marketed and processed food. The whole farm-to-table movement shows consumer interest in sustainable practices that benefit society, farmers, and better health and nutrition for consumers.

Still other movements have given rise to alternative ideas of consumption and marketing in attempts to escape consumerism altogether. The Burning Man Project, the Mountain Men rendezvous, and Rainbow, along with virtual online worlds such as Second Life, reveal a level of consumer activism that is generating alternative communal movements against the individualistic orientation of consumption in society. Investigating these movements demonstrates to anthropologists how sites or outlying events can both serve as escapes from mass commercialization or act as turning points for new consumer experiences.

For instance, consumer researcher Robert Kozinets studied The Burning Man project (2002), which is a week-long annual event held in the Black Rock Desert in Nevada. Kozinets attended the event and discovered that while it is alleged to epitomize a free, bonding community among participants, it also represented a collective form of resistance to commercialization. While brands like General Mills and Dove ice cream bars were given out as free food samples, the power of the "gift ritual" was about not charging for items. Gifts belong in the realm of mutually caring and supportive relationships. Although the brands are commercially sold elsewhere, in this context they evidenced an anti-commercialism ideal that promoted a communal bond. Moreover, narratives collected from participants revealed a nostalgic longing for an "uncontaminated past" of purer personal relations, imagined from an earlier "idealized" past.

Burning Man also hosts an art festival. The circulation of craft goods and handmade items further created a sense of nostalgia for past close relationships. Participants described a sense of a caring community associated with art, and that art generates the "best in society." The communal ethos that Kozinets found in the festival appeared to resist an established order and instead, if only temporarily, imagine a community apart from the commoditized world. Understanding romanticized views of consumers, involving gift exchange, art circulation, and a desire for deep community relations lets firms design alternative experiences for consumers, such as what is happening currently in the rise of craft-oriented ventures.

Anthropologist Grant McCracken in *Return of the Artisan* (2022), charts the recent emergence of an American artisanal movement that is shifting from the margins to the mainstream. Prompted by post pandemic malaise, he claims disillusioned workers are leaving regular jobs and learning to become cheesemongers, bakers, jewelers, and more. Artisanal life appears to offer a sense of control and liberation from office routine, while online sites such as Etsy become main sources for launching new business ventures. This coincides with the launch of Amazon's "Handmade," which offers a site where artisans from over 80 countries are selling their craft on Amazon.

These movements interest anthropologists, since what began with the rise of "micropreneurs" (entrepreneurs operating on a small level) and nostalgia for personal relations at artistic festivals like Burning Man, now appears to be evolving into a new artisan economy that may redefine the ways consumers work and shop. Such movements reveal the potential for studying consumer behavior and consumption, where consumers attempt to alter capitalistic practices, adapt its use, or reinvent the basis of community participation. The relationship of consumer research to these new ideas, trends and movements is shown to be a continually evolving cultural process that anthropologists continue to investigate.

NEW VIEWS TO CAPITALISM AND CONSUMER RESEARCH

Besides tracking various social movements in market conditions, anthropologists are also re-examining alternative views to capitalism. Capitalism assumes multiple forms, from Anglo-American stock market capitalism to welfare capitalism practiced in Japan, Germany, and the Nordic countries. Nigel Thrift (2005, 2) contends that capitalism itself is always changing; highly unstable, "unfinished," in constant flux, uncertain about the future, and yet dependent upon it. A new kind of "soft capitalism" is emerging, he claims, "continually harvesting ideas, renewing people, reworking commodities ... in an attempt to harness creative energies for its own sake" (2005, 16–17). The rise of soft capitalism signifies "both this new formation's adaptive characteristics and its sup-posedly caring, sharing ethos." The new capitalism is more reflexive, thoughtful, and aware of consequences, spawning a set of environmental, social and governance (ESG) values that shape most commercial enterprises and which also leads pedagogical knowledge production in most business schools today.

Consumer research shows the growth and importance to society of a new ethos in corporate responsibility. ESG values are shown to be as important to firms and consumers as they are to society. They show how corporate values of ESG can guide corporate actions to benefit society as well as hold corporations accountable for their actions. Companies traditionally measured value based on accounting metrics of revenue, profits, and losses, but, after the 2015 Paris Climate Agreement, ESG values came to the forefront of business accountability. ESG metrics might include measuring the energy a company takes in and the waste it discharges, the resources it needs, and the consequences for people as a result; or the relationships a company fosters with diverse people and the institutions it nurtures in communities where it does business, and include a focus on labor relations, diversity, and inclusion. In 2020, 92% of S&P 500 companies produced a publicly available sustainability report, up from 20% of firms in 2011. This represents not only a move towards a more accountable and responsible form of capitalism, but also capitalism that is more attuned to consumer perceptions and consumer demands for more corporate social responsibility and public good works.

Capitalism is not only more likely to be held accountable for demonstrating corporate responsibility to the public but is also more dependent on consumer ideas for manufacturing innovation into its products and services. MIT professor, Eric Von Hippel (2005) notes that individual innovations to products and services, developed by actual users, are often freely shared and better designed, creating communities of user-innovation and rich intellectual commons. For example, kite surfing is a water sport in which the user stands on a surfboard, and surfs the waves while holding a large, steerable kite. Manufacturers came in with products as the market grew in the early 2000s. However, a fan base developed an on-line community in 2001 to increase social interaction among users. Members shared patterns for kites and added helpful hints and tools for kite design. One design added foot straps attached to the surfboard base to allow users to hang on with their feet for better control and jump over waves without falling off. Other user innovators joined in and posted improved designs. The scale and quality of the collective user effort grew to exceed the original manufacturers designs, indicating that user-centered innovation offers greater advantages over manufacturer-centric innovation systems. Increasingly, manufacturers rely on users for innovation and so conduct consumer research to understand users' points of view. This movement of firms increasingly dependent on users and consumers for product ideas and innovation also coincides with new views on consumer research, which have shifted in recent years to be more collaborative.

THE COLLABORATIVE TURN IN CONSUMER RESEARCH

Sarah Pink and her co-authors argue, "unless anthropologists are prepared to build bridges with other disciplines and practices … anthropology is unlikely to flourish as an active and influential discipline" (Pink et al. 2017, 5–6; see also Malefyt and Morais 2012, 149–154). Fortunately, for decades, practicing anthropologists have collaborated in and with "agriculture, development, education, marketing, medical researchers and clinicians" (Pink et al. 2017, 10). Anthropologists working in and for business describe how they collaborate in teams with other researchers, brand managers, designers, engineers, advertising creatives, and so forth, to accomplish negotiated ends with clients. This process presents a substantial shift from the previous model of fieldwork in academic anthropology, where the lone researcher sets out in research and assumes a singular authoritative voice for his or her people.

Anthropologist and consumer researcher, Maryann McCabe, describes the "collaborative turn" in consumer ethnography, which occurs from recent changes in consumer research that include participation with respondents, bringing clients along in research projects, and from correspondence with other anthropologist colleagues. This reframes business anthropology and its method of participant observation "as co-constructed or co-created experience" (2013, 160). Collaboration in consumer research offers anthropologists a new way of thinking about ethnography as it reshapes the process of doing ethnography. Fieldwork is more inclusive of the respondents themselves, who become an essential part of the production of knowledge.

From this perspective, fieldwork learning is not an individual activity and knowledge is not something picked up along the way.

Rather, "learning is an inevitable part of participation in social practices and happens in the pursuit of joint enterprises" (Berg and Fors 2017, 62). This invites us to think about fieldwork as a process of interviewing *with* others and doing a specific practice *with* someone else, and about knowledge as something you *become part of* with others by participating in the practice. Participant observation then becomes a commitment to learning by doing, in a process of becoming educated by being "in" the experience with others. Partaking in the activity and becoming a social actor in the social worlds of our interlocutors, is what makes consumer research anthropological in its approach.

This occurs with fieldwork that is conducted online as well. For example, Tricia Wang (2014) details her approach to data gathering in a process called, "live fieldnoting." In this, she uses social media tools to establish and maintain relationships with participants, empowering them to feel they are truly participating in research, instead of just responding as informants. Developing ongoing dialogue with her audiences produces new forms of data, extending narratives, especially after meeting them in interviews. Far from "treating people as objects of investigation" or "assigning them to categories" or "explaining them away" (Ingold 2018, 131) Wang's fieldwork data is co-produced, subjective, and participatory with her informants and grows from practical engagement *with* them.

RESEARCHING CONSUMERS ONLINE IN THE DIGITAL AGE

Researching consumers on social media offers anthropologists a valuable way to access and understand cultural meanings, holding that culture is created, lived, and shared online just as it is offline (Miller and Horst 2012). Studying social media habits of various individuals and communities provides an inexpensive, accessible way of engaging consumers at different moments in their daily lives. Researchers note that social media are not all alike, and that the proliferation of apps, sites, and platforms offer consumers a range of specific tools and resources to help foster different social groupings while offering individuals a means to express themselves. Indeed, the type of social media people use tends to structure and shape the type and depth of social interactions in ways that organize their social space and flows of interactions. Culture studied online reveals the shared meanings that give coherence to people's lives; and while online culture is made visible through following individual actions, its meanings are still inherently social and collective. This presents anthropologists with a new venue in which to explore shared cultural values, common belief systems, and various patterns of behavior in a digital context.

STUDYING COMMUNITY DYNAMICS ON FACEBOOK

For instance, Facebook made a major change in 2017 to support online communities, giving users the tools they need to build communities on its platforms, shifting from the original focus on connecting family and friends. Facebook made changes to its product for people to engage with others who share their interests, like putting Facebook "Groups" front and center on the app experience. But Facebook needed a better understanding of how groups or small communities form, and, more specifically, how people experience and build community.

Calen Cole and Carolyn Wei (2020), two consumer researchers, conducted ethnographic research for Facebook in 2019 to better understand the needs of different types of groups and the ways that technology platforms support them. Academic perspectives, they discovered, typically focused on communities organizing in response to a problem. In addition, communities are often assumed to be pre-existing homogenous units, defined by geographical area or common demographics. Moreover, studies of online groups have often focused exclusively on virtual communities. Their research took a different approach.

They focused on how groups live in both worlds, offline and online, and how this balance shifted depending on the group's primary orientation. Beyond groups forming due to some problem or homogeneously by geographical or social unit, they explored communities that were formed, joined, and abandoned voluntarily from a "grassroots" effort. In the setting of Madrid, Spain, they chose a multi-method approach. They ran mobile diaries before in-person fieldwork to sense group relationships and ensure a mix of group type; they conducted in-depth interviews with people; they observed immersions of community spaces and group meetings to sense the cultural context. Finally, they conducted brief unscheduled intercept interviews in public spaces to compare their sample representatives to the general population. This mix of online and offline research patterned the lives of the groups of people they sought to study.

Their research found that many groups had different dynamics, and community growth meant different things. For only a few groups, growth was a priority. Other groups sought to limit or even avoid too much growth; these groups sought instead to increase the richness of the experience for their existing members by elevating the stature of the group, or by increasing engagement with an outside audience. The most significant finding was understanding how group needs varied depending on the purpose of the group and on the stage in development of the group. As a result, they identified three main toolkits that community groups could use for support from Facebook technology, and this would help build better groups.

TIKTOK FOR SELF-EXPRESSION

Other studies by consumer researchers investigate how video hosting services, such as TikTok, can create positive outcomes for certain populations that otherwise are limited or excluded from social media participation. Consumer researcher, Stuart Henshall (2019), discovered that the widespread adoption of TikTok is expanding cultural opportunities for self-expression and creative work in illiterate communities that other platforms previously restricted and excluded new consumers.

In this research for Convo, a qualitative research and strategy firm based in Mumbai and San Francisco, he observed online an older, non-literate Indian woman using Google Assistant to access recipes. The woman expressed great satisfaction that her family would be eating meals created by her, and that they would appreciate her more. This woman, he surmises, may later become a creator of recipes and videos over time, despite her not being able to write. By creating new video content without needing to write, the woman would effectively bypass the need for text, bringing her a new sense of independence.

Henshall is hopeful that this app and future designs may provide significant social change. For the less literate, talking to a mobile assistant (an AI built into a service, like Google Assistant) and using TikTok video services allows a new range of people to access recipes and creates a new zone for experimentation and inquiry. Previously, sharing recipes across time and space required writing, and less literate users avoided doing anything much more with their phones than calling. Now, voice and video technology are catalyzing new forms of engagement with a wider world, creating new possibilities among less literate populations, and reframing what happens on mobile devices for everyone.

For UX design purposes, Henshall sees an opportunity to redesign how software and apps are developed over time by rethinking how people will use mobile devices in the future, with these new users in mind. The implications for anthropologists are to challenge the dominance of text and allow less educated people to express themselves across public, private, formal, and informal communications.

CONSUMER RESEARCH IN ADVERTISING

Advertising is still the primary means of paid communication by which companies promote their products, brands, and services to consumers. Advertising agencies seek to infuse their clients' products and services with cultural significance, converting commodity objects and services into symbolic images and narratives that have relevance for consumers, based on an understanding of consumers' everyday lives. The goal of anthropologists doing consumer research for advertising agencies is to understand the ways that brand messages represent and connect with their target populations to influence purchase and help build brand loyalty. But the ways of reaching and communicating to audiences for advertisers has drastically shifted in recent years, making the investigation of consumer agency even more urgent for researchers.

Advertising through traditional media, such as television, radio, and print, is increasingly supplemented by new digital media on internet channels, apps, and social platforms and the various devices such as smartphones, laptops, and tablets that enable these media. These new media offer advertisers a more interactive field in which to engage consumers, not only for messaging, but also for conducting consumer research. Communicating brands on social media, for instance, helps advertisers facilitate exchanges between consumers and producers because digital media is more personally directed to individuals, involving communication that is two-way, interactive, and immediately responsive.

Ethnographic research with consumers and their relation to brands on social media also offers a means to interpret changes in social messages, such as gender or racial stereotypes, and ascertain ways that consumers adapt messages or resist them, sometimes even incorporating conflicting messages. When this occurs, paradoxical consumption practices that emerge in research can offer insights into how consumers integrate commercial discourses with their own experiences or how they resist. For instance, is wearing make-up for women (and men) something prohibitive, patriarchal, merely objectifying the wearer in the gaze of others, or is it liberating, self-authenticating, and self-empowering? In discussions with women on a research project for a cosmetic brand, we heard both opinions expressed, sometimes at the same time, by the same women.

PARADOXES OF CONSUMER BEHAVIOR IN MARKET RESEARCH

In an ethnographic project for Revlon cosmetics, research showed that women users of cosmetics may, paradoxically, hold two conflicting cultural views simultaneously. Women may resist cosmetic advertising discourse, which focuses on the importance of outward physical appearance, while at the same time incorporating and transforming such views within their own make-up practice to connect inner and outer beauty concepts for the self. In the investigation we conducted for Revlon, conflicting ideas about self, relationships, and others in evaluating, absorbing, and contesting advertising messages became evident in consumer research.

Revlon enlisted my services for a consumer research project, along with Maryann McCabe and Antonella Fabri, to gain insight into the self-transformation that occurs when women put on make-up in their everyday routines (see McCabe et al. 2017). Our research involved in-home discussions with 28 women in friendship groups, consisting of a host and three friends, in two US cities. Women in the study were given a make-up kit supplied by Revlon and interviewed in friendship groups twice, once before and once after experimenting with make-up products in the kits.

Participants kept journals on their beauty rituals and made collages showing perceptions of self before and after applying make-up. Participants were 25 to 49 years old, married or single, hetero-sexual or homosexual, and Caucasian, African American, or Latina.

Participants told us that morning make-up routines play an important role in making them feel more confident and prepared for the day and interacting with other people. Feeling good con-nects with looking good and creates an authentic self. For partici-pants, wearing make-up does not alone generate feelings of self-worth but expresses the inner worth they feel and helps maintain feminine identity. Insofar as participants blend inner feelings of beauty with outer expressions of beauty in the embodied experi-ence of applying make-up, they resist cosmetic advertising dis-course, which privileges external appearance and the gaze of others. Yet, paradoxically, participants subscribe to cosmetic advertising discourse about looking good because, on infrequent occasions when they are not wearing make-up, they feel incom-plete, not fully "put together" and embarrassed about their physical appearance. Thus, participants revealed how women manage their bodies and negotiate identity in the social context of gendered hierarchies, and in relation to material products (brands) that assist them in creating an authentic self.

Revlon subsequently produced a narrated film about our study and aired it on a YouTube channel. The social media film resulted in a high number of views and positive comments, reflecting greater consumer engagement with audiences than traditional tel-evision commercials that Revlon had produced concurrently. The social media film was more effective than the traditional ad because, in part, it followed real couples and delved into women's insecurities and self-doubts about themselves and their partners. It also cast couples in a narrative on how developing a reflective sense of trust in self (using make-up and following self-affirmation guidelines for a week) made women feel more confident, which improved most couples' relationships with their partners. The creation of the online "love stories" from real couples were more powerful and successful than the national television ads that pro-moted beautiful models, because online engagement encouraged greater interactivity from consumers on social media searches, blog posts, and organic shares and comments with others. This finding affirms the powerful influence and benefit to corporations of consumer and brand interactions on social media, and how anthropological thinking helped direct consumer research.

Grant McCracken (2005) identifies brand communication to consumers as a "meaning transfer process," in which products and services become saturated with cultural meanings that are transferred back to target audiences through advertising, based on how consumers use products and services in their everyday lives and the meanings that they imbue. But reconsidering branding in light of the widespread influence and interactivity of social media, perhaps social interactivity reconfigures the meaning transfer process of brands as *more collaborative* between producers and consumers than previously considered through one-way traditional media. Brands today are far more subject to interactivity and co-creation by the confluence of consumers, marketers, and trends on various online platforms of social media than in the past. The rise of social media influencers in marketing has also greatly empowered consumers to express themselves, form communities, and replace traditional "top down" advertising with co-created participatory messaging from the "bottom up." This shift requires researchers to understand consumers' evolving relationships to brands and their community of followers, as anthropologists studying the interactions of online groups helps firms develop a more negotiated brand meaning for products and services.

ANTHROPOLOGICAL IMPLICATIONS FOR CHANGE WITHIN COMPANIES

> The meanings revealed in the interpretations we co-create with our informants are not merely edifying, they are thrilling ... (especially for) practitioners whose insights are translated into breakthrough brand strategies, creative new products or services, compelling advertising campaigns, improved customer journeys through more engagingly designed servicescapes, practical and humane organizational restructurings, cogent expert witness testimony in product liability trials, or any of the countless other managerial or civic interventions that anthropological or ethnographic perspectives enable.
>
> (Sherry 2017, 46)

The contributing actions of anthropologists conducting consumer research to enhance our understanding and lobby for reformation of practices in corporations, as John Sherry recalls above, is encouraging. The reconfiguration of business priorities to experiment with and adapt ethical guidelines and practices, especially incorporating ESG values, enriches anthropologist's opportunities and ability to bring cultural practices *into the world* of business to help transform it. Sherry adds, "The monolithic view of firms as nefarious is not ethnologically viable ... Recent experiments in corporate social responsibility, cause-related marketing, and triple bottom line accounting, among others, suggest that firms can become effective contributors to the common good" (2017, 51). Along with changes in capitalism and increased consumer activism through social media participation, corporations are becoming more open and flexible to incorporating concepts and practices that adapt guidelines for more responsible social actions. Business anthropologists, more than ever, are empowered as facilitators to effect change within and across organizations.

As anthropologists, we may take for granted our approach and ways of understanding people; yet, it is still often novel and path-breaking for businesses to know their customer up close and personally, especially with the rise of, and dependence on, digital marketing and big data analytics. Among the perspectives that make anthropologists valuable partners for innovating and implementing positive change, as discussed throughout these chapters, are our holistic way of thinking, etic–emic understanding of people, and crucial reflexivity on actions and impact on others.

Cultural analysis in consumer research encourages businesses to understand their consumer in new ways in relation to social systems in culture, to reflect on themselves, and to uncover emergent opportunities. Applying critical reflexivity to question a company's perspective of what's going on may inspire employees to wonder about ways they might be misreading or misrepresenting a target audience and even offer the organization a competitive advantage to change their perspective. Providing an emic perspective helps companies acknowledge that consumers have their own perspectives and practices in using products and services, which are often taken for granted by brand managers too familiar with their own brand to see it any differently, and holistic perspectives help managers integrate new understandings back into the corporation for broader implications. By raising awareness of, and highlighting, the cultural depth of consumers' lives, consumer research can provide the space for discovery and deeper connection beyond other research approaches and become a crucial tool for advocating strategic change from within. For example, change in perspective is what occurred as the result of an insightful ethnographic study of men's shaving rituals for the Gillette company.

CHANGING CORPORATE PERSPECTIVES OF CONSUMERS

Gillette, a men's grooming and hair-care company, approached me at BBDO to conduct in-home interviews among men who regularly shaved (see Malefyt 2014). Gillette was puzzled over reports of contradictory behavior they received in connection with a new high end shaving product they recently acquired. They wanted ethnographic research to explain why the small segment of men who regularly purchased "The Art of Shaving," were strong advocates of shaving, when the majority of Gillette's target men disliked shaving altogether. The men who were high-involvement brand advocates expressed great satisfaction in shaving and using the premium product, when most men showed low involvement, disliked shaving, and completed the shaving task as quickly as possible.

We interviewed and observed 24 men aged 18–49 in the New York, New Jersey and Connecticut regions, half of whom bought the premium product, while the other half purchased a minimum of shaving equipment. We discovered that shaving, for the brand enthusiasts, was a highly engaging activity they enjoyed doing. Their daily grooming routine led them to feel like "better men" in what they described as a performance-oriented, competitive work world. Clothes, hair, and shaving played a key role in defining who they were in their "presentation of self" to others (Goffman 1959). Grooming not only transformed these men to be "ready for the day," but also identified them as men for whom care and attention to appearance was important. In this regard, their personal involvement with shaving translated into enhancing the social self.

But beyond solving a functional problem of removing unwanted facial hair in a daily grooming regimen that the company expected, their descriptions of shaving revealed a hidden sensory involvement with the brand. What we observed as a shaving routine was actually a brand ritual. Men who engaged in the shaving ritual showed greater focus, self-awareness and concern for process, they employed a different vocabulary of shaving terms, committed more time to the effort, and shared their thoughts and skills online with other men. None of these highly involved behaviors occurred with the other men we spoke to who used the "regular" shaving brand.

Our research initially confirmed what the company had already known, that normally shaving, for many men, was drudgery, "a chore" to be minimized or skipped, when possible. Many men only referenced the end result of a good shave in the absence of negatives (no nicks or cuts). Yet, for other men, shaving was a ritual in which the journey of shaving was cherished. Men described in rich sensory detail the importance of sounds, movement, and scents during shaving. Some played special tunes, like classic Frank Sinatra songs, while other men enjoyed the sound and feel of stirring the brush in the cup, "whisking it fast" and "frothing up the lather." Still other men attended to the light scraping sound of the blade held at just the right angle as it glided over their skin. For others, the choice among brand scents was evocative. Smelling Citrus Lemon, Lavender, Sandalwood, or Ocean Kelp demarcated a transition from unclean to clean (Howes 1987), or, in their terms, "to feel ready" for the day. Men also attended to the brand packaging with more acuity. Some spoke of the glass jar containing the moisturizing pre-shave lotion of the brand as being more "old-fashioned" and "genuine," than if it were made of plastic.

In the end, our learning about the sensory experience of shaving had identified a new way to look at shaving that the client had not foreseen. Our study helped develop a new marketing strategy for the high-end shaving product, suggesting that certain men might appreciate effort in shaving as part of a grooming ritual. The ad campaign focused on the sensual aspects of shaving, affirming men who embraced shaving as savants, experts, and connoisseurs of grooming. The "Art of Shaving" campaign reclaimed the shaving experience as a manifestation of one's performative skills leading to "the perfect shave," and designed for a select community of fellow shavers, a "brotherhood" who relished the act. It was the hidden, taken-for-granted sensory aspects of the experience that we revealed in consumer research, which led us to discover brand rituals in shaving as a key aspect of marketing the brand experientially.

Industry has its own ideas about how consumer markets work and mostly builds consumer relations ideologically around such notions. Corporate models of consumer decision-making often regard their brand users as individuals, based on theories of individual psychological motivation, even as they ignore the embeddedness of individuals in social systems. But this story of discovery of shaving rituals in consumer research and brand shaving communities that developed from online enthusiasts helped to foster change within the organization. New products were created that catered to sensory dimensions of men's experience, with lotions, balms, and fragrances. Positive change can be incremental, such as making small adjustments that enhance consumers' perception of a brand and increase their satisfaction with a product or service. Change may also inadvertently help foster thriving communities among shaving enthusiasts, where none existed previously, as occurred with the "Art of Shaving" brand. While anthropologists who work in or for organizations continuously struggle with attempting to have their work "fit in or stand out" (McCabe and Denny 2019), instigating change within corporations may best be evaluated as a matter of degree.

On a minimal scale, business anthropologists can reframe problems for clients and affect how clients address target audiences through improving marketing and advertising strategies, communications, or innovation—delivering on the promises and expectations of the brand. On a broader scale, anthropologists can simultaneously contest cultural ideologies perpetuated by business practices that help shape markets, and hope to direct meaningful cultural change, such as embedding ESG values that adapt corporate strategies for the greater good. Toms Shoes, for example, is featured in *Forbes* magazine (Morgan, 2021) as one of 20 influential companies that benefit others for social good. Toms originally based its business model on donating a pair of shoes to needy children for every pair purchased. The company shifted away from this model to allow for more freedom in how it donates. It consults with World Vision in Health, founded by anthropologist Paul

Farmer, and gives one-third of its profits to grassroots organizations that not only provide shoes for the needy, but also fight for causes including mental health, ending gun violence, and increasing access to economic opportunity, impacting over 100 million lives. Anthropologists can influence corporate models as consultants or work in corporations to direct purposeful change.

CONCLUSION: HOW CAN ANTHROPOLOGISTS BE AGENTS OF CHANGE?

Tim Ingold (2013, 13) argues that "… the ultimate objective of anthropology is not documentary but transformational …" He adds, "what value lies in transformations of the self if they end there, if selves do not go on reciprocally to transform others and the world?" While Ingold advocates for teaching anthropology as a way to impact others and change the world, I argue that cultural analysis in consumer research of products and services can be transformational in how we bring the meaning of things in the cultural world *back into organizations* in the form of insights, ideas, and stories we tell. This is how we can affect change. Jay Hasbrouck (2018, 93) concurs that bringing our insights into corporations and telling our stories to our corporate clients can help integrate perspectives from many different stakeholders in an organization, especially when they coincide with the firm's guiding principles, mission, and purpose statement. Then, "ethnographic depictions can bridge the gap" that often exists between corporate ideals and cultural realities of people's experiences with products and services, making real change occur.

As this chapter has shown, anthropological research of consumers in social media, advertising, UX studies, and more has taken a turn from the detached objectivity of its predecessors to subjectivity, participation, and co-creation in producing collaborative meaning for products and services. This means the anthropologists' input in delivering consumer insights has more of an impact in creating meaningful change within ad agencies, for corporate clients, and in other industries. The shift in ethnographic fieldwork and perspective from the participant observer as objective sole authority to co-creator and collaborator with interviewees, colleagues, and business partners also calls for a reconfiguring of the formal etic study of the consumer as a hard target market object, into a more subjective emic understanding of consumer markets as living active participants that co-create culture with others. Opportunities in business today encourage anthropologists to get involved, lend their views, and challenge the ways firms may contribute to sustainable growth or social justice in society.

Conducting consumer research, whether for advertising agencies, UX research, or as a consultant for corporate clients, demonstrates the ways business anthropologists are advancing positive change in society. Morais and Malefyt (2010) suggest that business anthropologists can instigate change from within firms but must first learn not only the models that corporations use, but also the language and culture of their corporate clients, as they would learn the language and culture of their informants in the field. By understanding marketing and business terms, metaphors used, code-switching behavior, reading body language, and the cultural dynamics of power in play, they will better connect with their clients' ways of thinking and improve their own chances of business success. As such, anthropologists may better adapt to the challenges of working in corporate environments, even as many corporations have their own codes of ethics in addressing proper and acceptable behavior towards employees and other stakeholders. When these approaches are adopted, anthropology in consumer research has a better chance of engaging in new circumstances, remaining relevant, and instigating change in the world for the greater good.

ORGANIZATIONAL ANTHROPOLOGY

Anthropologists who work in or for business organizations, whether as employees, consultants, or partners, seek to understand cultural groupings within institutions from an anthropological perspective. According to Ann Jordan (2019), organizational anthropologists help to solve work-culture issues and better understand the nature and functioning of the organizational structure from within and across the entire organization. The anthropology of work and organizations as a field of study within business anthropology spans a variety of organizations, from for-profit and non-profit organizations, financial corporations, small and medium scale businesses, family run businesses, government agencies, military organizations, educational institutions, labor unions, indigenous organizations, virtual and digital organizations, and health care organizations.

While the size, scope and type of organizations differ, modern organizations face similar challenges when addressing issues of management, work processes, mission fulfillment, and implementing innovation and change. Anthropologists help organizations understand issues internal to their organization and assist firms in managing change, and help firms understand the ways they can improve their work practices with partners, negotiate and trade in different environments, and positively impact their local communities, nation-states, and even world economics and politics. As such, organizational anthropology is about how organizations incorporate, manage and, at times, improve global processes. This chapter discusses the relevance of applying the anthropological concept of culture to different organizations and discusses how anthropologists apply useful dimensions of culture to help organizations adapt to change.

DOI: 10.4324/9781003358930-4

Anthropologists working in and for organizations understand businesses as cultural systems in themselves, such that business organizations can be viewed as complex entities with mini-cultures, subcultures and cross-reference groups, composed of various people with different roles, statuses, and value systems. Forms of culture are expressed in employees' shared values, behavior patterns, and communication styles, and become evident in employee gatherings at common workspaces, meetings and workplace-based interactions, and even schedules. Importantly, the culture of a firm helps employees, from the clerk to the CEO, both feel and express a common identity that is essential to ensure that all people of the company are united in their efforts. Business anthropologists note how successful firms maintain a common cultural identity by integrating symbols (corporate logos or names), legends (origin stories, stories about past success or failures), heroes (influential figures from the past), communication patterns (language, phrases, non-verbal cues, traditions and rituals), shared values (what the firm stands for, its mission and purpose), patterns of social interaction (norms of behavior, dress codes), rules to follow (work processes and procedures), and shared experiences (team projects, stories of success or failure, familiar rituals and habits).

STUDYING UP AND STUDYING DOWN: WHY ANTHROPOLOGISTS SHOULD STUDY ORGANIZATIONS

In 1969, Laura Nader famously challenged the anthropological community to reinvent itself with a startling premise at the time: she claimed we should "study up" rather than "study down."

> How has it come to be … that anthropologists are more interested in why peasants don't change than why the auto industry doesn't innovate, or why the Pentagon or universities cannot be more organizationally creative? … What if, in reinventing anthropology, anthropologists were to study the colonizers, rather than the colonized, the culture of power rather than the culture of the powerless, the culture of affluence rather than the culture of poverty?
>
> (Nader 1969, 289).

In raising these questions, Nader set a formal agenda for academic anthropologists to turn their attention to the critical study of formal organizations and places of work in American society and beyond. As a harbinger of business anthropology, her call to action was to make what was familiar strange, since "It is the corporate form that encases us in our daily life," and yet its ubiquity also remains invisible to us (Rose 1989, 6, in Schwartzman 1993, 2). Since then, the anthropology of organizations has blossomed into a growing field of practice and consulting for many business anthropologists. Indeed, anthropologists seek to understand organizations holistically, not piecemeal as Nader suggested. Anthropologists in organizations today study corporations from the lowest classification level to the highest, and everything in between, to the extent that it is possible.

Ironically, earlier US studies of industrial organizations that occurred in the 1920s and 1930s are mostly forgotten or were dismissed, even as now the value of several key studies legitimize the importance of using ethnographic investigations to understand workers and their role in industrial plant behavior. Between the years 1920 and 1960, when anthropologists engaged with business institutions, their efforts were dismissed, considered irrelevant and from which it was thought little could be learned (Baba 2012). Yet, in acknowledging these previous investigations, we find that it was during this early period that both academic and practitioner anthropologists established the foundations for current business engagements, including the widespread use of ethnographic practice in industry, design studies, and consumer research, as well as in critical reflections upon anthropology and business. Moreover, during this early period, anthropological engagement with business interests set in motion patterns of interaction that became institutionalized over the century and gradually defined business anthropology as a discipline.

REVISITING TWO EARLY NOTABLE INDUSTRY STUDIES

Anthropology applied to the study of contemporary society in the form of "studying up" is noted in two famous studies of organizations. The first is the psychological work study that was intended to improve worker productivity and efficiency in the Hawthorne plant; the second is the investigation of the social stratification of a community and the resulting labor strike at a shoe factory in Yankee City.

The widely known Hawthorne study, conducted in Chicago in the 1920s, forms one of the "creation myths" of industrial psychologists and sociologists even today. It began as a test of the scientific management principles associated with Frederick W. Taylor and his efforts to improve industrial efficiency. Ironically, the actual study disproved many of Taylor's principles and "discovered" informal and "naturalistic" studies of human behavior. As a result, a new research tradition emerged in the human relations school.

The study initiated at the Hawthorne plant, a supplier for the Western Electric Company, intended to investigate the relationship between fatigue and monotony, and job satisfaction among the 29,000 workers at the plant. However, investigating the workers' habits produced startling results that baffled researchers. In the experiments, researchers noted a general improvement in the output of workers, but which rose independently from the specific changes made to working conditions. Oddly, worker output rose even when the specific rewards were withdrawn from the experiment. It was suggested that merely attempting to listen and attend sympathetically to the workers themselves, as well as giving the workers being studied attention, which also gave them status, might explain the increase in worker productivity. Researchers realized that the presence of the researchers themselves had a direct impact on shaping worker productivity. This has subsequently been known as the "Hawthorne effect." The study was significant at the time because it represented one of the first ethnographic accounts using direct observations and interviews with workers to gain information, challenging Taylor's management and efficiency theories, and giving support to the psychological and social needs of workers. It stressed human relations as essential to creating good working conditions, thus founding the human relations schools of management.

In another notable project of industrial significance, a group of human relations researchers sought to understand the underlying social conditions of industrial workers at a shoe factory in Yankee City, Massachusetts, in the 1930s. The project used ethnography to examine the social stratification of a community. The researchers rejected predetermined social class indicators based on income, education, and housing, and instead used direct observation of social group formation and conducted interviews in the factory and the community. In a novel approach, they examined not only the internal dynamics of working conditions of a shoe factory, but also the broader community context of the factory, to situate the historical context of industrial conflict that resulted in a workers' strike. Applying this broader analytical framework, the researchers were able to relate the reasons for the labor strike to changing factory production conditions, poor labor relations, the increasing mechanization of the factory, and the resulting loss of control and alienation that the workers felt. This study had a great impact, since it went beyond simply considering shop floor conditions and included a larger examination of the economic, political, and social forces that were transforming the nature of relations between capital and labor.

These early studies showed the importance of ethnographic techniques in gathering data and joining them with anthropological theories of human behavior. They helped universities found programs such as Human Relations in Industry studies, and helped contribute to our understanding of how workers interact with each other, as well as management, in specific job situations. Beyond human relations investigations of industrial labor, the anthropology of work and organizations currently involves research into issues of workplace dynamics that helps mitigate conflict and alienation among workers, exploitation of workers and worker response, and addresses issues of power inequalities between workers and management. The anthropology of organizations emphasizes the importance of ethnographic methods for developing new, responsible frameworks that continue to address these issues in the modern-day workplace by studying the dynamics of culture within an organization.

CULTURE APPLIED TO ORGANIZATIONS

Corporate culture is a popular phrase used by myriad experts to discern and differentiate the type of "culture" or workplace environment a particular firm holds and instills for work practices among its employees. But often, the reference to culture has nothing to do with a holistic understanding of a firm's implicit and explicit set of rules, values, beliefs, and practices across the firm. Specialists such as industrial–organizational psychologists and industrial sociologists frequently apply the term "corporate culture" to help determine an organization's operating ethos and corporate values, which they analyze to supplement management techniques to improve leadership in firms. But culture, from this perspective, is used as an organizational tool at the macro level that can help manipulate the efforts of its leaders, and which often applies a top-down approach to instill a desired set of corporate values in managing an organization.

In contrast, business anthropologists understand culture as residing in the human interactions at every level within institutions, as they study all the components of the organization's structure, reward systems, implicit and explicit rules of behavior, shared goals, and flows of power that are learned and shared as parts of that firm's culture. While there exist multiple definitions of culture, for anthropologists working in organizations, "culture" can simply be defined as an integrated system of shared ideas, thoughts, ideals, attitudes, behaviors, and material artifacts that characterize a group. As such, culture exists in individual organizations across the globe and is shared, learned, symbolic, and adaptive. Anthropologist Tomoko Hamada Connolly suggests culture "is an amalgam of historically derived meanings that include values, conventions, artifacts, norms, discursive practices, power-relations, and institutional habitus, which together constitute daily social realities for individual people" (Hamada Connolly 2015, 125).

Importantly, an organization may not have a single culture but, rather, one that consists of a web of interacting cultures that can be internally nested, cross-cutting and overlapping, and the organization is itself a subculture within larger cultural units. A global company, such as General Motors, operates multiple vehicle units globally, as well as runs a finance division, a fleet car service, trucks, along with engines and other strategic business units. In addition, within an organization, individuals are members of ethnic, regional, gender, and professional groups outside of the organization. Thus, cultures in institutions are learned, shared, and negotiated, and not dictated by leaders as a set of preferred values. Every individual worker contributes to multiple cultural groupings in the organization and, along with the CEO, is a "culture producer." Power is never absolute, since subordinates create culture and hold power just as leaders do, although typically not to the same degree. For a business organization, the organizational culture needs to be adaptive to the internal and external environment just as an agricultural culture adapts to its natural environment and changing climatic conditions. A rigid, slowly adapting culture cannot survive or be successful in a fast-moving environment. Anthropologists in organizations help firms respond and adjust to change in a rapidly changing global market economy.

HOW ANTHROPOLOGISTS HELP BUSINESS NAVIGATE CHANGE

According to Jay Hasbrouck (2018) "ethnographic thinking" applied to corporate culture helps provide an interpretive lens that offers new ways to see how cultural worlds are organized, as it also offers a framework for thinking about how cultural worlds are formed and how they evolve and interact. Hasbrouck (2018, 16–24) describes the value of anthropological thinking in corporations as expansive in helping to find higher up patterns for sense-making approaches. This way of thinking addresses the "why" of corporate situations instead of a reductive process, such as the popular "design thinking" process, which seeks to refine and home in on problems to offer a solution. The anthropological approach is more strategic, rather than seeking mere implementation.

Hasbrouck further claims that corporations can be thought of as "ecosystems" (2018, 17) in which a wide range of behaviors constitute the culture of an organization. Ethnographers of organizations may consider a range of information to analyze when investigating what constitutes a particular corporate culture, which Hasbrouck (2018, 17) locates in:

> body language, interpersonal interactions, behavioral triggers, contradictions, unspoken priorities, normalized practices, sequences of events, affinities, attachments, repellants workarounds, social transgressions, implicit hierarchies, priorities, neglected people/places/things, as well as honored people/places/things, displays of comfort or discomfort, unconscious practices and habits, and interactions with material goods.

Each of these artifacts and behaviors create and affect the culture around people and places. Anthropologists' ability to sort out and prioritize levels of significance in these contexts is what under-standing corporate culture is about. Workplace cultures are full of unspoken boundaries and implicit rules for behavioral norms. When someone at work violates an unwritten rule and is faced with reactions from others, it indicates, either directly or indirectly, that either speech or behavior is inappropriate in that setting. But also, the reactions of those who respond to the transgression indi-cate that something has gone wrong.

Anthropologists become aware of such nuances in workplace behavior, since norms and orthodoxies within an organization often go unspoken, and drive hidden dimensions of workplace practices that have a direct impact on day-to-day business decisions. In one example, Hasbrouck (2018, 21–22) details how, as a consultant to an organization in trouble, he immediately sensed indications of inter-nal corporate conflict when junior staff members asked to conduct their personal interviews with him outside the workplace setting. As his investigation of workforce culture progressed, Hasbrouck noted other patterns of discord in that senior leadership, while attempting to be sincere and attentive, in fact was very rigid, hierarchical, and unsupportive of suggestions for work-culture changes. In addition, it appeared that senior executives acted as gatekeepers of old approa-ches, actively working against cross- departmental collaboration and embracing new approaches to business. As a result, junior-level staff built up a level of skepticism, and, over time, developed a sense of resignation towards senior management and implementing change to improve the organizational culture.

To help implement change, Hasbrouck attended a special task-force meeting where he observed various levels of interaction between senior executives and junior staff members. One senior executive commented that junior staff members were unprofes-sional and that when asked to contribute creative ideas to help the organization, their ideas were just unacceptable. Other senior executives affirmed this critique. But what Hasbrouck also noted was that senior leadership offered no help to mentor junior staff or guide them in idea development. This frustration expressed by senior management simply affirmed an existing void between senior and junior staff levels.

As Hasbrouck continued in his workplace investigation, he identified three implicit norms within the organization that furthered this cultural divide between senior and junior levels. First, senior management deprioritized communication that was open, honest, and direct between senior and junior staff members. Second, the use of educational pedigree or seniority among senior executives was leveraged to dismiss new ideas and potential innovation among junior staff; and third, senior management held strict control over information and, in particular, budgets, which created an atmosphere in which junior members felt discouraged, distrusted, and unable to work collaboratively with others. In this context, change for the organization would be nearly impossible to implement. Power relations were embedded within organizational norms, preventing the staff from embracing creativity, openness, collaboration, and new ideas. Hasbrouck brought awareness to these insights and helped the organization address these implicit cultural norms, while simultaneously developing new norms and practices that were built on shared values among all, and a desired future state for the organization.

HOW ANTHROPOLOGISTS HELP BUILD CORPORATE CULTURE

In *The Culture Puzzle* (2021), the authors, Mario Moussa, a business consultant, and Derek Newberry and Greg Urban, both anthropologists, discuss the importance of corporate culture from an anthropological and management consulting perspective. They claim corporate culture is not merely an add-on, but that business success begins and ends with the culture of a business. Culture, as anthropologists use the term, is a process of learning and adapting to change that begins when a subculture or "tribe"[1] is formed. The culture of a business sustains the human need for relationships as a tribe is formed, allowing for change and growth, identity, sense of belonging, and creativity and innovation to flourish. The authors specify four areas of a business culture that need attention to help sustain a healthy, vital corporate culture. They are vision, interest, habit, and innovation. Their blueprint for successful organizations borrows directly from anthropological ideas of culture and is applied to business settings, not from a top-down approach of forcing change but growing and responding to cultural tendencies from the ground up, which form in the workplace as people spend time among fellow employees.

First, they discuss vision as an essential force of corporate culture in a business environment, built on the idea that people in a tribe need a community that stresses shared values and beliefs. This is shared in a corporate setting in mission and values statements, in strategic plans for a company, in credos and mottos, on websites, speeches at town hall meetings, in the formalized rules and standard operating procedures, and other ways of publicizing an organization's culture. But more than that, this vision of values and beliefs is shared collectively in stories that people at all levels hear in their company's history.

THE POWER OF STORIES IN FORMING CORPORATE CULTURAL IDENTITY

Stories are essential to cultural transmission of information, but also of sentiment, pride, identity, and sense of belonging to companies. Origin stories of a company establish a context for current social behaviors and, as coworkers hear about the stories, they are likely to share them with others. Embedded in the stories are common sub-themes, or threads, that run through the collection. They provide important clues to what people really think and how they should act. As such, stories change over time since they capture the richness of multiple voices and various experiences at different moments in time. Variations in stories told are essential and typically build around, or modify, the key elements of the main story. By adapting stories to changing conditions and incorporating other voices, they become personalized and express employees' sentiments and a connection to others in the present situation.

For example, one origin story that was revisited and strengthened helped a company restore its culture, purpose, and success in the marketplace. LEGO was once the pre-eminent toy manufacturer, controlling 80% of sales for construction toys and which consumer surveys ranked among such household names as Disney and Nike. However, by 2004 it was losing market share, with profit margins operating at negative 30%. Cutting management staff and costs to streamline processes and tighten up efficiencies did little to stem the losses. In *The Moment of Clarity* (2014), authors Christian Madsbjerg and Mikkel Rasmussen discuss using anthropological analysis and ethnographic research into LEGO culture, which revealed that the brand story had gotten lost. The turn-around success of LEGO led by ethnographic insights showed that the company's focus and new product development should not be on copying the rise of digital toys that offered instant satisfaction to children, but, rather, as research had shown, be based on the need for creative, deeply involving, craft building of toys. A generation of children who played with digital toys actually enjoyed the adventurous, self-driven sense of developing mastery that hours of unsupervised LEGO toy building offered. Hands-on play of crafting clever structures and figures was LEGO's advantage over the instant gratification of video games. Researchers discovered in conversations, not only with consumers, but also with employees, that this brand story had existed in the culture of LEGO and needed to be reactivated in the company mission of "Inspiring the Builders of Tomorrow." Reviving this story of LEGO helped employees follow a future vision and business success for the company.

Anthropologists take stories as an essential part of all culture. Stories give contextual relevance to facts in the present and are accommodated to fit the larger meaning of the story. Indeed, in corporate forms of storytelling, fact and fiction are often blurred, so that report, gossip, history, legend, and myth may be partially invented but are also intended to be understood as factual parts of a story. The way people in a firm may depict any one segment or sequence of a story is related to the whole, and, thus, becomes a new story, according to anthropologist Edward Bruner (1986). As such, past, present, and future are constructed as fictions that are understood to be factual. Stories may also embed themselves in other stories or themes that are relative to context, occasions, and experience, and shift over time.

For example, Bruner discusses in US history how, before the Second World War, the narrative of Native American acculturation shifted from portraying American Indians as the romantic exotic to later, in the 1960s, when Native American resistance depicted American Indians as victimized. Stories are the basis for social movements and political agendas. The earlier romanticized narrative attempted to legitimize the acculturation of natives into US culture through the ideal of the melting pot. However, as this narrative shifted dramatically to reveal persecution, it sought instead to pre-serve and dignify native culture and folklore. Stories operate not only in the mind as ideas, but also have a basis in experience and social practice. As social sentiments change, so does the narrative and meaning of the story.

SATISFYING INTEREST AND CREATING TRIBES WITH PASSION

The second dimension to building a successful corporate culture, according to authors Moussa, Newberry, and Urban, is to tap into a corporation's tribal passion and sense of purpose. Anthropologists have long studied the ways humans seek out forms of belonging to a community. People in a company at all levels associate with others who share a similar feeling and pursue a common goal with others.

Tribes often cut across organizational charts of companies. Within a company, nested subcultures, such as educational soft-ware sales, may be nested within software sales, which then is nested within general sales. But there may be cross-cutting groups, such as administrative assistants that band together with other assistants from different departments but in similar roles. There are also tribal tendencies of collaboration and competition, such that small groups band together and form silos: marketing competes with accounting; both marketing and accounting are pitted against research and development. Group affinities and conflicts thus criss-cross an organization, but can also be rallied by common passions.

In *The True Believer* (2010), Eric Hoffer describes how successful social movements appeal not only to people's heads, but to their hearts. People are inherently emotional, which causes a "soul stir-ring, spectacular, communal undertaking" (2010, 18). People are joined together not by their ability, or even competence, in something, but by a shared passion, and passion is required for a movement to succeed. Something is asked of them, and they are allowed to feel vested in the movement. This insight initiates many social, political, religious, and cultural movements.

For example, Howard Schultz returned as CEO of Starbucks in 2008, when the company was facing bankruptcy. He assembled 10,000 store managers in New Orleans in attempts to rally a movement to save the company. Before the assembly of store managers in a Superdome stadium, he presented the firm's situation as a crucible of survival, as in rallying the troops in an emergency. He transformed the loose collection of factions into a "tribe of tribes" (Moussa et al. 2021, 115). The shared vision he offered was passion, reminding them of their shared connection, orienting them to a common goal, and giving them something to do by returning to what made Starbucks great in the first place. He set in motion their mission statement: "To inspire and nurture the human spirit— one person, one cup and one neighborhood at a time."

In other words, successful movements frame their goals as a mission or "noble purpose" with a moral basis that workers can identify with. The success of the televison program *American Idol* is explained in large part by its democratic and meritocratic underpinning; it reflects an America where talent is recognized and where the collective will of people rewards success. Employees in a company, likewise, rally around common goals and bonds are strengthened through the collective work they do. Importantly, markers of collective purpose are found in articles of faith, uniforms, symbols, esoteric rituals and language, and the network infrastructure across which people can communicate. The esoteric nature of many of these practices strengthens the sense of shared unity and purpose in a company.

CORPORATE CULTURE IS BUILT ON THE FORMATION OF RITUALS

The third element of forming a corporate culture is to tap into corporate rituals and make them more prominent. Rituals in organizations are essential because they serve as a communication and learning system that helps channel the thoughts, feelings, and behaviors of members into pro-organizational pathways (Malefyt and Morais, 2010). Rituals are also understood as ordering devices, producing status and prestige for groups, and, importantly, constituting cultural templates for subsequent action and the interpretation of behaviors.

For example, rituals are crucial to the structure and function of advertising agencies. Ritual offers an ideal construct for analyzing the multiple roles and transformations of various employees that define advertising agency collaboration and creative innovation. Robert Morais and I have argued that, in certain creative industries, such as advertising, ritual offers a framework that helps organize and motivate the employees and partners involved to collaborate towards a particular end: ritual occurs within a set time frame, with a set of performers, and requires an audience, a special place and occasion of performance (Turner 1987, 23). These elements constitute the observable and functional aspects of ritual, but also evoke the symbolic dynamics of social drama in which innovation occurs for advertising agencies.

Importantly, the transforming work of ritual requires a tension between two vital agency efforts—the "Account" team, which represents brand stability and company permanence, and the "Creative" team, which represents creative change and brand innovation—in moving the company forward. The Account team maintains the stability of the agency's relationship with their client, which metaphorically translates into stabilizing the brand itself. The Creative team members, in contrast, see their work on the brand as a way to express their talents and innovative thinking: they desire to change the brand so that they and the brand gain popular and professional recognition. The Account Planning team, distinct from the Account Management team, draws new material for this mediating work to happen from the consumer landscape, where different and sometimes challenging perspectives on the brand need transformations even before reaching the agency. Thus, the brand, the subject of the agency's relationship with clients and the object of creative efforts for success, needs ritual to mediate these three forces—trends from the consumer side, agency–client brand stability, and creative dynamics for brand change.

To reconcile this tension into a workable structure that is productive to agency life, innovative creative work, client security, and keeping abreast of new trends, advertising agencies depend on rituals of presentations for all three elements to converge. When this happens, ordinary products are transformed into elevated brands. Thus, the collective efforts of employee teams work to resolve tensions, leading to creative outcomes that secure future work from the corporate client while stabilizing the agency.

When a successful pitch leads to securing a new client, the outcome can feed into the collective story-making-process that strengthens the agency community. The story also helps elevate the multiple hidden groups of people working behind the scenes of a pitch to make it a success. This includes a range of employees—from those in the production department, who select image and typesets, clean up details, and print the ads, to administrative assistants who coordinate schedules with client agendas, to janitors and kitchen staff, who set up the meeting room and food/beverage accompaniments. All celebrate and share the win as an expression of corporate culture and community pride.

TAPPING INTO INNOVATION TO BUILD CORPORATE CULTURE

A fourth dimension of building corporate culture comes from tapping into company innovation. Successful organizations must continually adapt and change as environments change, internally and externally. As such, organizations need to embrace and foster processes of innovation that help them grow and adapt to change. It can happen at the tribal level, as Elizabeth Briody, Robert Trotter and Tracy Meerwarth (2010) wrote about from observations at General Motors (GM). In the mid-1980s, while GM mandated a Total Quality Management initiative companywide to improve performance of factories and keep quality as central to work, implementing this effort was difficult to practice. Briody noted, in ethnographic work on factory floors, how workers were afraid of mistakes: covering up errors and not taking blame was essential to survival there. Yet, fear of blame compounded the issue of workers not receiving the spare parts they needed to keep up the pace. Workers felt they couldn't complain, since this seemed like a form of blame on management. So, Briody witnessed a clever innovation—to do their jobs properly and keep up the pace, teams began to find and hide extra parts they needed, skillfully creating an informal system of exchange that helped decrease production line stoppages. GM workers had cleverly developed a creative workaround that, through tribal connections, formed an alternative system to get work done and help solve issues themselves. Briody subsequently wrote that creativity can operate "below the radar" of senior management and help form a community, rather than sparring with each other for limited resources. This informal system of exchange of workarounds not only displayed worker ingenuity, but also showed how innovative ideas often come out of the work itself.

This latter idea builds upon Tim Ingold's idea of innovation, that true creativity is relational and collective, and is done through engaging with the people, objects, and materials that surround a given situation (Hallam and Ingold 2007). Rather than starting with the standard psychological definitions of creativity that tends to emphasize novelty as its defining feature, Ingold and Hallam (2007) say creativity and even imitation are not formulaic or mechanical processes of making or duplicating something, but always involve *improvisation*—making adjustments, working with material properties, making adaptations that fit the needs of the situation. The search for objective solutions in a short time is what provides the impetus to generate ideas. This impulse is creativity channeled and works as a stimulus for organizational transformation to provide a creative practice in the search for solutions, causing some initial disorder that is subsequently reorganized into new formulations.

Thus, a comprehensive understanding of the norms, values, customs, and dynamics in the workplace itself, can help the anthropologist identify the most effective catalysts for innovation. Also, focusing on innovation from employees themselves helps identify the pathways through which new ideas can flow and thrive within the organization. This provides insight into the ways that employees can co-evolve the lived experience of the company's story by understanding how their own personal values and experiences can align with innovation. Ascertaining who are the key people who help influence the flow of interactions and determining the power dynamics in those channels will help anthropologists to see how insights live beyond just ideas.

MANAGING POWER RELATIONS AND INNOVATION IN CORPORATIONS

When working with companies to assist them in developing employee programs that help them foster innovation and idea generation for the firm, Hasbrouck (2018) discusses how inevitably you encounter issues of power and difference. Ethnographic work is particularly useful in this context for understanding organizational behavior among workers at different levels, and how work with them exposes the often informal or hidden ways that power flows through an organization. In many organizations, employees in lower positions, such as administrative assistants, secretaries, line workers, and so forth, appear to simply execute commands of those "higher ups", or the key decision makers, whose job it is to direct and manage a firm. The formal hierarchy establishes an organizational chart that disseminates the flow of command down the chain. But, as Hasbrouck notes, in reality people who occupy lower positions often do have power in their ability to "control the pace" (2018, 50) of information flow and also to distribute information as to where and how other people may receive it. As such, power resides in how they may prioritize and assign different values to distributing information in a timely fashion and shape the perception and urgency of initiatives as it is handed down to them by their superiors.

This subtle expression of power is shaped with their experience in an institution, as we may encounter savvy admins who "know the ropes of the system", the back doors, so to speak, to get things done. This would include knowledge of workarounds, workplace traditions, short cuts, seasonal changes, people to avoid, games of seek-and-hide, people to align with, and other "soft" information that helps workers and administrators complete their agendas. The existence and acknowledgement of these informal systems of power merges and works with the behind-the-scenes of more formal systems of power, so the researcher understanding this is key to understanding organizational behavior that can determine the success or failure of many initiatives instigated by leadership of an organization.[2]

As Hasbrouck mentions, gaining trust with respondents so that the ethnographer becomes aware of these pathways is essential to understanding how the formal and informal flows of power work together. Understanding how informal power flows within an organization can be useful for breaking up silos that inhibit growth and communication among workers, by leveraging existing pathways already in use or creating new pathways that may channel unrecognized flows of power. In another sense, working with pathways can help an organization shift its priorities, from holding up formal structures of power that might inhibit communication to rewarding actions that work to support and build shared values among employees. This is also a way to tap into sources for employee innovation and generating new ideas, since innovation works better through informal "hidden" networks than through formal hierarchical structures of power.

Hasbrouck maintains that formal hierarchies are created to maintain and rigidly enforce power flows, whereas informal networks are flexible and adapt to changing circumstances through the context of social interactions (2018, 52). Formalized power seeks to maintain order, and dissent, whether direct or informal, is typically discouraged, since it is taken as a threat to the stability of the organization. Informal networks, on the other hand, are important to the growth and change of an organization, since they are based on interactions that are fluid. If a strong set of shared values permeates the culture, informal networks are better at innovating and adapting to changing market conditions than formal hierarchies. This was shown in the example that Elizabeth Briody discovered among GM line workers, who created a vast informal trading network from being innovative, without the awareness of top management. Anthropologists working in businesses are, thus, a great source for recognizing these informal networks and helping companies achieve organic growth and innovation where possible. When workers feel empowered in an informal network, they will often get the best results by innovating for themselves.

Solutions for companies often come from the resources of their employees, and ideas can lead to designing human-centered training programs, pairing an employee who has an idea with an innovation team member who can act as an internal consultant. Ideas can be collected and sorted out to be further developed by a company sponsored internal incubator that partnered innovative ideas with an entrepreneur working in the same space. An innovation team, writes Hasbrouck, could use ethnography to gather such ideas from people on the ground and in the trenches, and strategically identify, expand, and drive innovation within the company.

Moreover, because employees work closely with products that a company offers, they are more likely to come up with inside knowledge to adapt or modify new products or processes to match changes in the consumer marketplace. One opportunity for executing this is to tap into the existing consumer user base of a product or service through social listening and getting ideas from a consumer base that feels included in company innovation. The larger marketplace has become an open forum in which consumers play an active role in creating and adapting the value of a brand they use. They have become a new source of competence that companies can tap into for their knowledge and experiences. This is how Starbucks engages tens of thousands of customers to innovate products and store experience.

For example, Starbucks has leveraged open innovation forums such as MyStarbucksIdea.com to draw creative ideas from customers in refining products and store experiences. As of December 2016, the website had received over 150K product, 55K experience, and 30K involvement ideas. In its first five years of the program, the company implemented 277 ideas, including digital awards on the Starbucks card and free in-store Wi-Fi. Through this initiative, customers helped introduce new varieties and flavors, such as skinny beverages, hazelnut macchiato, and pumpkin spice flavored coffee. The inventory of over 200,000 ideas, which continues to grow, provides management with both short-term tactical and long-term strategic initiatives. Getting ideas from customers has allowed Starbucks to innovate and roll out new products, improve the in-store experience and keep its customers engaged.

FROM PARTNERSHIPS TO MEETINGS: COLLABORATION AS AN EXPRESSION OF CULTURAL ORGANIZATION IN CROSS-CULTURAL WORK

As Gary Ferraro and Elizabeth Briody stress in *The Cultural Dimension of Global Business* (2023), partnership lies at the heart of global business operations and are successful when they bring together people, ideas, resources, and shared vision. Partnerships require participation of at least two parties who share the same goals and objectives. They vary greatly, examples being between an entrepreneur and supplier, a large corporation and several suppliers, an entrepreneur and a family-owned business, and a consultant may partner with a client firm. Partnerships, thus, take on various roles and forms depending on mutual interests, availability and expertise of key personnel, allocation of resources, and the urgency and scale of the effort. Partnerships, write Ferraro and Briody (2023), come with fundamental challenges for business anthropologists to work with, since, for a partnership to be successful, they must overcome differences in cultural ideas and practices of organization and implementation. This is where the anthropologist can help bring awareness to subtle and glaring issues that might impede successful partnerships. Some obstacles have to do with ideas of status and power, intergroup dynamics, building trust (or over-coming the lack thereof), flows of knowledge, constraints on learning, or even misconceptions about the partners efforts and differences in management styles.

Effective partnerships depend on the principle of collaboration and agreement between all participants involved. This means agreeing upon the ability of the two (or more) partners to work together and solve problems. Effective partnerships exemplify strong relationships which are built on high levels of cooperation, commitment, and trust. Briody and Trotter define partnerships as "collaborative arrangements, in which participants enter into rela-tionships, combine their resources, time, and expertise through the various roles they play, and work towards the creation of new knowledge, products and services" (2008, 7, 196).

The most basic of organizational activities that anthropologists observe and help participants to improve and achieve effective partnerships is the business meeting. Meetings are an essential part of any business, since it is where people gather in an event to share information, exchange ideas, start projects and initiatives, and keep an organization moving towards achieving common goals and objectives. By one count, there are around 55 million meetings held each week in the United States alone. On average, employees in any given business participate in at least eight meetings per week. Clearly, meetings are integral to most organizations, where the potential for issues or conflicts when joining work colleagues, clients, and business partners who work in different locations or organizations is extremely high.

Importantly, culture affects how meetings are conceptualized, managed and integrated into the organization. The issue of orga-nizational culture is compounded when working with partners cross-culturally. Differences in meetings become apparent to attendees when looking for cues in how a meeting is run. For instance, the format of the meeting can depend on issues of culture and affect. What is expected depends on cultural background, and affects who does the talking—as in one leader, or a group of participants, or are all participants expected to participate equally? Furthermore, meetings in different cultural settings with various cultural participants determine who presents material, offers ideas, and whose views seem to matter most, and how participants or select individuals keep the meeting moving along.

Anthropologists, such as Briody, identify the roles that meeting participants play, the amount of planning associated with the meetings, the extent to which the agenda is followed, and what ultimately occurs when the meeting concludes. One interesting area when looking at the influence of meeting style is the dimension of national culture on the character and structure of the meeting. National cultural styles impact the composition of the meeting participants, how participants prepare for the meeting, how likely it is to proceed, and what the follow-up tasks are likely to be. National culture also affects differences in power and social status within each organization and among the participants of a meeting. Nevertheless, the work of Briody shows that organizational culture plays a more significant role than national culture in shaping business practices of meetings. It's vital to understand the relation between corporate culture and the culture of participants when examining the influence of meetings.

In 2013, Elizabeth Briody was asked to assist in a cost-saving measure for General Motors in the development of a car seat that could be shared across multiple platforms of vehicles in the US and beyond. The focus was on joining various groups in meetings from three different car units in different cultures to discuss design and implementation of the car seat. Briody was invited to participate in the meetings by the chief engineer, who oversaw the development of the seat across the three different car units. She sat in on 23 meetings and was allowed to observe and take notes of the intergroup dynamics. She also conducted follow-up interviews with the chief engineer, and one with each of the engineers from the representative car units.

Meeting attributes, such as the purpose of meetings, differentiated the partnering organizations, writes Briody. For the German organization, the purpose of the meeting was to make decisions. For the American organization, the purpose of the meeting was to reach consensus. The amount of time allocated to the meeting was another attribute that distinguished German from American meetings. Both kept time in meetings to a minimum. However, in American organizations, much of the working week was spent in meetings, equating meetings with work, while the German organization did not think of a meeting as counting for work. The German organization placed high value on structure and organization, while, for the American organization, the content of the meeting evolved.

Briody observed very different dynamics in the meetings, so it appeared that all three units would not agree on a common car seat design across all platforms. One of the issues Briody identified was that each car unit was autonomous within the corporation and was accountable for generating its own profit. This made it difficult for the engineer of each unit to compromise, but instead each engineer sought to minimize cost even at the expense of the other units.

On another level, cultural differences again played out in work practices. The US car unit worked directly with its parts supplier so that all technical specifications for the car parts were accurate early in the design process, otherwise they would have to compensate the supplier for any changes made later in the process. For the German car unit, the team routinely made modifications in design throughout the process and did not have to specify them accurately at the beginning. Since the supplier "worked for them", they were not expected to compensate them for changes made along the way. The results of these different ways of working with partners from the American and German factories caused conflict in issues of reporting changes, assumed responsibilities, and willingness to learn about cultural differences and change behaviors to accommodate all.

Briody stepped in as an anthropologist to make recommendations. She first advised the corporation to include the impact and importance of negotiations among units as a factor when weighing the costs and benefits of the single seat design. She also advised the corporation to strengthen its commitment to overall project management, rather than pay employees through their individual units, and request that the corporation compensate them as a unified and collaborative project. Another recommendation was to bring in cross-cultural representatives to help train the units to better understand alternative points of view. Briody's recommendations resulted in specific advice on how vehicle programs should be structured differently, and this model was implemented in other cross-cultural challenges faced by General Motors.

OTHER EXAMPLES: ANTHROPOLOGISTS ASSISTING FAMILY-OWNED FIRMS AND HEALTHCARE SYSTEMS

Anthropologists look at other forms of cultural groupings to understand variations in organizations. Anthropologists find that the culture of small businesses and family owned and managed practices have their own system of rules and beliefs that differ from large organizations. Healthcare organizations, like hospitals and clinics, operate to serve the public but also to save patients' lives. While the concept of culture applies to all organizations, small businesses present their own unique challenges when anthropologists assess the firms' values, beliefs and practices.

Business anthropologists who work for small businesses and family run enterprises, oftentimes act as external consultants. In their consulting help, they typically examine the level of integration into the firm of the business founder's or current leader's personal values, vision, and behavior, the sociocultural milieu of the locality in the country where they work, and compare this to the dynamics among workers and stakeholders and the firm's identity, vision, and current leadership. Especially among small businesses that are owned and led by family members, the organizational culture is highly influenced by the shared values, identity, standards of behavior, and the founding origin stories that may lead to a small firm's stability, continuity, and business success or failure.

SMALL BUSINESS MANAGEMENT IN ITALY

Dipak Pant (2014) is an anthropologist who consults for several Italian small businesses. Family-run businesses in Europe tend to favor advice offered by generalists who gain consensus among family members and the local community, rather than from specialists or experts giving professional advice. Since more than 90% of Italy's roughly six million businesses are family owned and operated, and over 93% of those support fewer than 50 employees, the small family-owned business is the model he worked with. Nevertheless, since more than half of the family firms nationally in

Italy are actively led by a senior family member of 60 years or more, every year tens of thousands of family firms undergo inter-generational transition in management to another family member, for which he often consults.

During the time of his analysis and consulting work, between the years 2008–2010, Italy was undergoing an economic crisis. A severe recession, coupled with a credit crunch, heavy tax burden, and a climate of political instability at a national level, plus a crisis of confidence in the European currency, led to many business failures and unemployment. As an anthropologist, Pant used ethnography to observe and advise businesses and help them focus on sustainability, business profitability, employee wellness, environmental care, and social responsibility. As a consultant, Italian business leaders were looking to him for clarity and foresight. His strategy started with repositioning the specific organizational and operational needs of the family-owned and run businesses in the context of global competitiveness.

His approach to helping Italian small businesses succeed against larger multinational companies was to instill a social opinion mobilizing campaign called Terre di Cuore, or "Places that are in your heart." In this effort, he helped local firms place-brand their products and services with owner-led emotional stories and histories about how a family member overcame obstacles to establish a business, especially for manufacturers of food, beverages, and textiles, but also for construction and service sectors. He also helped small firms improve their businesses through changing the physical dimensions of workplace habitats, and the social and personal skills, knowledge, and relationships among workers.

External place improvements were the first area for Pant to focus on. He writes that raising the aesthetic appeal of the workplace buildings, courtyard, surroundings, and landscaping, and improving the eco-efficiency of material structures, encourages workers and stakeholders to develop a sense of belonging, identity and wellness. Visual improvements to the place suggest to employees and customers alike that the family-owned business matters and has a stake in the local community. This brings a sense of pride in locality and is a competitive feature that large multinational corporations cannot challenge.

Once workplace habitat revisions begin to happen, Pant claims it is then easier to improve workforce social and relational qualities, such as loyalty, skills, knowledge, competence, and coordination. External physical improvements start to generate anticipation of real change in the firm among employees. Then Pant recommends exercises in sharing work experience and company mission and vision, again joined with workers' own ambitions for an organization that helps in building and expressing origin stories. The collaborative foresight exercise is not aimed at predicting the future, but in raising awareness about possibilities, direction, and purpose with crucial feedback from employees. This process also brought attention to the organization's inner and intangible resources, such as shared identity, memory, distinctiveness, prestige, community cohesion and importance of personal relationships. This also added value to the organization by helping business leaders or owners to see the connection between employees and community.

Pant's implementation of strategy is especially fruitful for small business owners and managers since it relies on anthropological concepts of joining human capital with place-based local knowledge. It also builds on employees' sense of pride and purpose, so businesses are more likely to incorporate sustainable practices. Pant's premise, then, is that anthropologists can help small businesses achieve an ethical balance between business applications of success and profitability with a drive for sustainability, since this favors the ultimate interests of the community and the habitat at the local level.

ANTHROPOLOGISTS IN THE HEALTHCARE INDUSTRY

Anthropologists have also made inroads into leading business research practices in the healthcare industry. Anthropologists work in healthcare to improve the healthcare process, train health care professionals, improve patient education, help develop medical tools, employ marketing and communication to various audiences—patients and professionals, and a combination of these outcomes. Anthropologists work with public agencies, health industry marketing and clinical departments, health professionals, and patients' associations.

In one example, Elizabeth Briody (2014) shows how she helped transform a hospital culture by changing the discourse. Administrators from one large American hospital hired Briody to help them improve their patient satisfaction scores, and, ultimately, the overall experiences of patients during their hospital stays. Her work involved assessing a new communications technique, known as AIDET, an acronym reflecting five fundamentals of staff–patient communication.[3] While conducting over 101 hospital staff interviews, plus 46 observations with patients and family members, and attending over 51 staff meetings, Briody and her team saw various types of discourses, some hidden in plain sight beyond the assessment tool, that impacted the patient experience.

Briody observed a subtle form of discourse that was powerfully effective. It was a form of empathetic engagement, when patients communicated nonverbally, such as through the call button, or by revealing facial expressions of discomfort. Briody noticed a rhythm between patient and nurse with patient actions followed by nurse responses. Despite possible language barriers and poor health, a natural empathetic connection played an important role in improving social exchanges. This Empathetic Engagement Model of discourse had powerful effects on patients. Nurses would listen to their patients, talk *with* them (not to them), make them as comfortable as possible, and engage them in their own care while still getting their clinical tasks accomplished. In fact, these individuals integrated their knowledge of nursing with their desire to help people to create a patient-centric environment.

Briody and colleagues made several recommendations related to the formal implementation of AIDET discourse. First, they stressed that hospital leaders should continue reinforcing AIDET as a foundation for staff–patient interactions. They recommended sharing AIDET successes (e.g., via video, stories) with employees throughout the hospital to help in training and coaching, so it became a routine part of staff-initiated interactions. Second, they recommended heightening staff responsiveness to patient questions and concerns. Seeking answers to patient queries in a timely fashion, and accommodating patient requests when appropriate, should be part of each employee's job. Finally, they recommended creating a series of new initiatives to highlight the importance of Empathetic Engagement discourse between staff and patients, and among staff members. Staff–patient interactions were unlikely to become consistently empathetic, engaging, or patient-centered if interactions across the workforce did not become more collaborative and empowering. Drawing attention to the nonverbal aspects of discourse in hospital culture helped raise awareness of the value of transforming the hospital to become more patient centered in its approach to healthcare.

WORKPLACE CULTURE: INVESTIGATING HEALTHCARE WORKERS IN THE "SPACES BETWEEN"

Jay Hasbrouck (2018, 33–40) was also hired as a consultant to investigate and understand nurse workflow conditions in the context of medication distribution to patients in a hospital system. His task was to help minimize errors in medicine dispensing and identify opportunities for improvement. By one estimate, approximately 251,000 lives are claimed each year because of medical error—about 9.5% of all deaths annually in the United States. This staggering number is higher than deaths caused by stroke, accidents, or Alzheimer's. Hasbrouck's research sought to mitigate hospital errors by understanding the underlying stresses, mindset, and responsibilities of nurses on active duty.

While he and his colleagues tracked and shadowed nurses in their daily hospital routines, the researchers found they were limited in opportunities to speak with them to better understand their motivations and rationale, because of the extreme fast pace and busyness of their schedules. Whether in the form of requests from colleagues, phone calls, pagers, lab technicians, therapists, physicians, family members, or some other source, nurses were continually bombarded by questions or other interruptions at a time when their concentration and focus were most crucial. The nurses' first priority was attending to their patients. So, the researchers had to improvise and conduct spot interviews with nurses in the hallways of the units, as they moved between rooms and schedules. This approach, they first thought, was not ideal, but later it revealed important insights. Nurses' daily routines were highly unscheduled and unpredictable, and as the researchers' style of interviewing adapted to the nurses' movement, they realized the right approach was accepting a high degree of tolerance for ambiguity—being flexible and adaptable.

As it turns out, the "spaces between" (Hasbrouck 2018, 36) of hallways for spot interviews became highly satisfactory sites to access data. This revised methodology also involved going off-script, being flexible to adapt to nurses' busy routines, which also realized a main point of anthropological research: cultural relativism means there are many paths to achieve good research. What seemed hurried or abnormal to them, was quite normal to the nurses' daily life. By embracing ambiguity and acknowledging many ways to accomplish the same goal, Hasbrouck and his colleagues were able to come up with creative solutions for the nurses' busy schedules. During medication administration they suggested making workflow adjustments such as re-prioritization of tasks and roles. They also recommended instigating anti-confusion measures, such as giving each nurse a medication carrying device and a clear flag that indicated when the nurse was unavailable for any type of interruption.

Interestingly, in other studies of organizations, hallways and corridors have also been shown to be ideal "spaces between" where researchers have uncovered insights. Christina Wasson (2000) discusses discovering this insight for one of E-Lab's first clients, Steelcase office furniture manufacturer. She explained how, prior to working with E-Lab's ethnographers, Steelcase designers would simply create products by imagining how people in office settings would go about doing their daily work. Designers had a simple and static vision of particular configurations of office furniture, designed around use in meeting rooms and individual workspaces (such as cubicles). They gave little thought to hallways and other "in between" workspaces. E-Lab's ethnographic studies of office environments showed a more complex picture. Workers in offices used space in ways that the designers hadn't anticipated, such that hallways and other "in between" spaces turned out to be highly significant sites of work interactions. This insight gave designers new ideas about creating chairs and whiteboards that were more mobile, to facilitate employee interactions in these "in between" spaces. In this way, anthropologists help businesses see alternative ways of utilizing resources and even non-spaces to develop relativistic solutions to issues.

CONCLUSION

As we have discovered in this chapter, business anthropologists apply anthropological thinking and ethnographic practices to help organizations develop deeper understanding of their employees, work environments, relationships, informal and formal structures of power, partnerships, meetings, customer bases, and so forth. Ethnography provides researchers with a way to examine business culture from the inside out, helping businesses develop conditions and offerings that align with the best work practices. Since cultures are always changing, companies must continuously realign their offerings, challenge their own assumptions, and reflect on the rules, behaviors, and patterns they rely on to keep the firm running properly. Beyond this, business anthropologists can help organizations re-identify what makes them a tribe.

New York Times writer, Ligaya Mishan (2020), in "What is a tribe?", claims that even though it's a charged term, no other word helps express the power of collective identity that people seek out to call their own. Benedict Anderson's (2016) main concept of imagined communities likewise illustrates humans' powerful ability to not only imagine and create culture, but also to reflect on it and change it. Anthropologist Greg Urban (2001) also explores the idea of culture as a force for change in corporations and reflects on the reason why people create a culture, which is about culture. The idea of corporations adapting and modifying their culture for the benefit of belonging, creating a sense of identity, purpose, and satisfaction in life, shows that business communities are defined not by an individual's hidden interior life or self-centered goals, but by the outward gestures, the communal language, the rituals and markings that are shared, and by the tributes and passion that are directed towards common ideals of goodness and purpose—not by what makes people different, but by what makes them alike. Business anthropologists tap into this human potential and desire for work–life purpose and give it direction and a sense of constructive organization for fostering positive change in society.

NOTES

1 "Tribe" is used as a catchall term for many types of group formations that express a strong sense of identity and belonging among members, acknowledging that the term also has negative associations with colonialist overtones that many scholars condemn.

2 Anecdotally, I recall my own experience of "subtle power" in graduate school. I befriended the head secretary of our anthropology department office at Brown by volunteering to help her sort material, lift heavy boxes, and move books around the office. I understood her to be an expert in helping me acquire my degree. She later divulged detailed information to me about which faculty members would be good to have on my dissertation committee, which ones were conflictual and to avoid, and which ones would read my work in a timely fashion and which ones let work pile up. This was crucial "insider information" to my success in passing my oral exams and defending my dissertation.

3 A = Acknowledge the patient (e.g., smile, make eye contact), I = Introduce yourself to the patient, D = Indicate the duration (e.g., of tests, discharge process), E = Explain (e.g., reason for the visit, initial diagnosis) and ask if there are any questions, T = Thank the patient.

DESIGN ANTHROPOLOGY

Design anthropology is an emerging transdisciplinary field that offers anthropologists a unique form of knowing, doing, and collaborating on concepts that transform people's lives. As a subdiscipline of anthropology, and one of the most prominent fields of business anthropology,[1] it is attaining salience among practitioners with the development of its own concepts, methods, and research practices. Moreover, design anthropology has evolved its own distinct style and practice of knowledge production that has helped in theorizing mainstream anthropology. They both borrow methods and challenges from each other as they contribute to mutual development. Even as design anthropology comes into its own, it stems from two separate knowledge traditions and social practices from which it achieves its unique distinction as a form of practicing anthropology.

The first knowledge tradition that fashions design anthropology is, unsurprisingly, design. The field of design is pervasive in modern society with many practitioners and subfields, including industrial design, architecture, systems design, human-computer interaction (HCI) design, service design, strategic design and innovation, and participatory design methods. Design, according to Ton Otto and Rachel Charlotte Smith (2013, 1) "is a process of thought and planning and is often depicted in its universal human capacity to set humankind apart from nature." To design something, they claim, is to imagine an idea and plan it out, give it a form, structure, and function before carrying it out in the world. In other words, design is *creating with intention*. Design is ultimately social because its products and ideas as concepts interact with people. While designing may be considered a universal social aspect of human practice, it

DOI: 10.4324/9781003358930-5

varies considerably in its implementation across different societies and cultures, and with different purposes and intents. Design has become a distinct field for the specialists of designers, whether creating solutions for different social and economic challenges that are industrial, digital, market strategies, or service oriented. In our increasingly "built" environment, design has become one of the major sources of cultural production and a force for change in contemporary society.

The second knowledge tradition that design anthropology draws from is that of anthropology, which represents the comparative study of peoples, societies, and cultures in social contexts worldwide. The intent of anthropology is to provide a "critical understanding of human being and knowing" in the world they inhabit (Ingold 2008, 69). A key characteristic of anthropology is the development and use of participant observation as the dominant method of field research. Participant observation is the central method of gathering data in ethnography, and so involves the immersion of a researcher in a particular social setting to observe and document everyday practices in detail from first-hand experience. The researcher is the primary instrument through which information is filtered, so fitting in with the people studied and joining in their activities is essential to producing good fieldwork. An ethnographic study results in an ethnography—such as a written report or book, but also sometimes as a film or exhibition—representing a theoretically informed critique about a people in a particular social setting and cultural context. Ethnography is, thus, both a form of inquiry—the immersion in social life to understand and describe it—and a product: a final ethnographic account.

The major relationship between design and anthropology is through the practice of ethnography. From the late 1970s, designers became aware of the value of ethnographic methodologies, to get a better understanding of the needs and experiences of users and the contexts in which products and computer systems were used. Beyond the advantage of ethnography and participant observation used for data gathering purposes, design and ethnography complement each other as both theoretical processes of inquiry that involve the iterative and contextual process of discovery—a reflexive and fluid approach to questioning oneself and the relationships to others—that adapts and re-examines the situatedness of the inquiry itself. The mutuality of shared perspectives goes further; just like ethnographers, designers immerse themselves in real-life situations (even if only temporarily or performatively) of users to gain insight into experiences and meanings that form the basis for reflection, imagination, and design. Designs are also concepts that are social and connect people, hence the importance of anthropology in understanding relationships to people. According to Adam Drazen (2021) design is a social field that creates relationships between people based on thought and sharing of concepts. Concepts, in this sense, are both thought essence and material constructs that people interact with.

A wonderful example of how design affects human lives is found in Drazin's book (2021, 1–2) in his description of the iPhone box design. People experience this same designed box in which a new iPhone is packaged and sold, the world over. It is designed in such a way that for the user, it takes time to open. Pulling at the lid of the box to open it up requires a long, drawn-out pull, with a sliding-sucking sound, before the box lid finally opens, and the owner can access the new iPhone. This design is intentional. It creates a satisfaction in the opening, and connotes associations of something of well-made quality, while building a sense of anticipation for the phone, even before engaging and interacting with the actual phone itself. This represents a moment in life when human life, culture, and material thoughts come to the fore, and expresses how concepts can be social. The concept of the phone quality is transmitted through thought-design from the designer to the user, and users can share in the thought-design with other users who enjoy and may advocate Apple's iPhone with other users. Design is, thus, a social field that creates relationships between people based on thought and the sharing of concepts.

Design anthropology is also flexible and adaptable as it works across multiple environments and with a variety of people, from designers working together with consumers or end-users, designers, engineers, anthropologists, and programmers, as well as working in different environments and work processes, from ethnographic data collection in real life, to studio design and prototyping, to presentations and product demonstrations, mixing everyday domains and professional domains. Design teams are always thinking about what sorts of people will use their designed services, objects, events, and the things being designed may reciprocally be thought to ask of the user, what are people like? So, design anthropology moves people, knowledge, and understandings back and forth between sites and among people, in experimental approaches to an issue. Design is also heuristic: it does not try to achieve a perfect solution as its goal but offers a "best-fit" approach. Therefore, the process of designing is *iterative*, it adapts and changes as it goes along, incorporating contexts with social values in the process of designing and imagining possible futures for an outcome of the design.

DIFFERENCES BETWEEN DESIGN ANTHROPOLOGY AND ACADEMIC ANTHROPOLOGY

Nevertheless, there are clear differences between design anthropology and academically oriented anthropology which follow some of the general distinctions made about business anthropology and academic anthropology in other chapters. Academic anthropology serves as a basis for gaining knowledge and generalizing about people and their culture through critique and writing up reports afterwards. A "thick" descriptive approach in ethnography describes what has occurred before and what is going on in the present, and then anthropologists offer a theoretical written critique of the situation. Design anthropology, in contrast, applies methods in ethnographic inquiry and theories of cultural analysis to purposefully *transform* a situation in an *intentionally interventionist way*. While design integrates anthropological methods, theory, frameworks, and critique with design principles and practices to address an increasingly wide range of complex systems, it also specifically seeks to offer solutions to problems that affect contemporary societies, institutions, and organizations. For this reason, it is increasingly applied to intractable, difficult, and complex issues, which are also known as "wicked" problems, to find workable solutions, such as seeking sustainable green solutions or urban planning ideas that address our most complex social situations.

In contemporary (post) industrial and digital societies, design has become a distinct domain of purposeful activity because the workforce of designers offer a variety of solutions to address different social and economic challenges: they generate ideas for products that are mass produced by industry; they develop digital systems that perform new functions in workplaces and private homes, such as home and business monitoring systems that protect against break-ins, fires, and floods; they design services for public sector institutions, such as helping maximize public bus routes to low income neighborhoods; they create strategies for innovation in business and marketing; or develop plans for urban and rural renewal and sustainable forms of living, like repurposing old elevated train tracks into beautiful walkable green parks, such as NYC's highline. Design professionals are trained in design schools and other higher education institutions, as well as within companies, and are increasingly supported by a range of academically based design studies. In modern societies, with their emphasis on innovation and change, which are often considered as "intrinsic values" (Suchman 2011), design has arguably become one of the major sites of cultural production and change, on a par with science, technology, media, and art.

Another dimension of design anthropology that makes it different from traditional anthropology involves the process of collaboration. Design anthropologists rarely work alone, as is the norm in academic anthropology. Rather, collaborative work in design involves various levels of engagement and interaction with different disciplines and stakeholders, including designers, researchers, producers, and end-users. Design anthropology radically breaks with the solo anthropological tradition, as its practitioners work in multidisciplinary teams, acting in complex roles as researchers, facilitators, and co-creators in processes of planning, design, and innovation. Moreover, practitioners in ethnographic and design disciplines jointly discuss collaboration to create new forms of knowledge and expand on opportunities that arise from new learnings. To be sure, there is no single recipe for collaboration, but, rather, multiple modes of collaboration depend on configuring situations as they occur. Team-based design ethnography involves conducting ethnographic work across disciplines or across sectors with academics and other stakeholders, as well as involving research participants themselves. In some team-based projects, for instance, ethnographers work with designers, or designers work with engineers in particular sets of relations, showing a way of collaboration with different skills that contribute to different practices and knowledge perspectives to projects. And, in all cases, design anthropology is underpinned by intellectual collaboration that is likewise focused on ethical issues when directed towards creating interventions.

Besides instigating positive social change and collaborating with other disciplines, a third difference from traditional anthropology and the central purpose of design anthropology is to give shape to possible futures. Design is focused on the social outcome and is supported by processes and theories from anthropology that are seen as able to help achieve this. The act of designing itself pulls together insights from a contextual environment in the present with knowledge of what has occurred in the past. Juxtaposing past understandings with present conditions, design anthropology then hopes to reconcile issues and mediate design concepts for the future. The task of design is then to transform ideas, materials, and resources in the present and map out a plurality of possible futures. One of the challenges in design anthropology is to develop tools and practices for collaborative future making. In a sense, everyone designs who *intentionally* devises courses of action aimed at changing existing situations into preferred ones. Design, thus, operates within transitional or liminal space, between existing situations and preferred situations. The famed Spanish architect, Santiago Calatrava, describes this transitional space as creating a type of dialogue, between things in your mind and things that don't yet exist on paper. This temporal approach to problem solving, of interweaving past and present to imagine and help create possible futures, makes design anthropology valuable and unique to business anthropology. As such, design anthropology is different from academic anthropology, since it is committed to participatory design and collaborative engagement in ideas and projects that are transformative and purposefully interventionist and give hope for the future.

Perhaps design anthropology is the most controversial field of business anthropology when compared to academic anthropology because, in its approach to theory and practice, its prime directive is to be interventionist, transformative, collaborative, and future oriented. Traditional anthropologists may be critical of design anthropologists for breaches in ethics—placing commercial clients at the forefront of agendas. Yet, design anthropology may also best represent the strongest discipline for championing hopeful possibilities, for imagining, designing, and co-creating real options for sustainable futures, based on social justice and virtuous cycles of growth. Design anthropology is not only future-oriented, transformative, and interventionist, it is founded on ideas, principles, and practices of "doing" and "making," rather than merely critiquing social problems as academic anthropology is accustomed to do. Its purpose is to design and create products, processes, and services that make a difference and that transform reality. Success can then be measured by how well it accomplishes these goals, rather than by the validity of its generalizations and critiques of culture.

ETHICS AND ACCOUNTABILITY

The foundational practice of design anthropology is inter-disciplinary, interventionist, and future-oriented, so that ethics and accountability are perhaps even more essential to help design anthropologists work collaboratively with others and establish responsible practices that "do no harm" while attempting to "do some good." Part of that responsibility is learning to work together with various people and other stakeholders. Design is supported by practices of reflexivity and ethical accountability, collaboration and participation, critical involvement and future-oriented interven-tion. The process of doing and making in design anthropology calls for an ethical responsibility to commit to engaging ethnography and participants as a form of revealing and intervening in the par-ticularities of everyday life, but also engage in the possible futures that may contest and challenge issues raised in social, economic, and political systems. A future-focused form of responsibility requires embracing uncertainty and risk of possible future events and circumstances that are unforeseen, and embracing failure when it occurs. Since ethics in design anthropology is always situated, contextual and project specific, there are a range of ethical and responsible responses to situations, depending on the project that is worked on.

Since design anthropologists work on a range of projects, ethical techniques do not necessarily exist pre-planned beyond the moment in which they emerge in projects. Like a performance, techniques come into action *as they occur*, "in the making" (Ingold 2013), as designers incrementally learn and adjust procedures in a way that is iterative or heuristic. For instance, Adam Drazin's (2021, 72–73) investigation of a post-socialist Romanian town in the 1990s shows how his analysis of material culture *in action*, led to new awareness of cultural concepts of gender roles like "care."

Drazin talked to Romanian people, but beyond talk, he observed women doing the "invisible" housework of cleaning to care for the family. He also noted the recent western influx of new soaps, cleaners, shampoos, floor cleaners, and other "care products" that were used to create new forms of social changes, such as Mother's Day gifts of soaps, teenagers experimenting with body scents, homeowners seeking new cleaning products and opening their homes to others. He interpreted "control over cleanliness" as a new way for women to exert control over their situation and over children and partners. Researchers thus acknowledge that insights occur in progress, in the doing, and as coming into being in forms and modes that are inevitably shaped by contingent circumstances in which designers, anthropologists, planners, and others engage, but often cannot predetermine.

Feedback is essential, adapting to situations on an as-needed basis such as in interviews, observations, video-recorded shop-along (where a researcher accompanies a consumer while they browse and shop for items, asking questions as the experience moves along), collage work, and other techniques. The goal again is not to aim for the perfect solution, but one that fits a best-case scenario. This process draws on the anthropological quality of being highly attentive and reflexive. This quality of reflexivity is essential to ethical ethnographic work, since a self-reflexive stance helps business properly understand what else they and others are experiencing in the world and provides a comparative way of looking at things. A self-reflexive stance thus examines conclusions, values, and the work impact they have on projects and in the world.

Being reflexive not only accounts for the immediate relations of ethnographic fieldwork but also the ways design anthropologists become attuned to the environments in which they practice. In what ways do designs impact the world by the turns, trends, modes of accountability and commitments of the time? As design anthropologists work with diverse partners in projects, they also constantly must make choices, and, as theoretically informed, they lean on a particular theoretical focus to guide them through issues. Should a particular project attend to a gendered focus? Should the sensory modes of engagement and embodied experiences influence and direct design analysis and intervention? Would a better decision in the research design involve empowering respondents themselves and enlist auto-ethnography? Should researchers conduct ethnography online and remotely, as happened during the height of the Covid-19 pandemic? As Sarah Pink and colleagues posit, "a design ethnographic technique is equally part of our research sites as anything else, but it is also part of an infrastructure for doing ethical and responsible design ethnography" (Pink et al. 2022, 23). A theoretically informed reflexive design approach encompasses these types of decisions in the forms of research, sharing, and interventions designers wish to produce. Concepts and practices of reflexivity and accountability thus become inseparable as one informs the other and both are bound up with ethics.

An example of dealing with an issue of accountability that design anthropologists frequently encounter when conducting user research is how to handle discrepancies between what people say, or might claim about themselves, and what they do in reality. How do researchers mediate and reconcile inaccuracies and inconsistencies in a responsible manner that works with users and leads to insightful knowledge? Anthropologists are responsible to observe carefully and listen closely to users, seeking larger patterns of behavior and looking for the unifying logic that makes sense of human behavior when encountering inconsistencies or contradictions.

DESIGNING A BREAKFAST FOOD

As an example, anthropologist Susan Squires (2002) led an investigation for a new product development based on motivations of mothers when buying food products for their children's breakfast. A two-phase study was proposed wherein, for the first phase, a focus group was held in which a representative selection of mothers responsible for feeding their families participated. During the focus group, mothers around the table were asked what was most important to them and for their children at breakfast time. The mothers gathered insisted that the most important part was that they feed their children healthy food. As one mother was quoted as saying: "I only feed my kids whole grain, nutritious food. Gives 'em a good start to the day …" (2002, 109).

Nevertheless, the ethnographic follow up in phase two found a different dimension of behavior. Susan Squires and a team member visited the same focus group respondents' homes at 6:30 a.m. and discovered a different reality. Squires observed that despite the claims of mothers in the focus group insisting on giving their children a healthy breakfast to start the day, the reality of the morning chaos contrasted with the mothers' good intentions. As many of the women juggled work with home responsibilities, most mothers hurried their children to school. Despite one mother's incessant efforts to get her two children to eat the healthy breakfast she had prepared, one child ate a bowl of surgery cereal before rushing off, and the other child left without eating anything. The healthy breakfast she had prepared was dumped down the garbage disposal. The researcher decided to follow up on the child's school routine and found out that at 10:00 a.m. the child that skipped breakfast was hungry, forcing him to open his lunch box and eat its contents. The child had developed a strategy for eating breakfast outside the home, but then had no lunch. Susan Squires understood the contradiction between what the mothers ideally wanted and the reality of their busy lives. This helped Yoplait, the yogurt food brand that sponsored the study, discover what was really happening and create a healthier and portable breakfast option: Go-Gurt portable snacks. In its first year of launch, Go-Gurt obtained $37 million in sales and is still today a popular breakfast option in countries such as the United States, Canada, Great Britain, Australia, and Japan (Squires 2002).

The practice of design anthropology thus involves multiple techniques of reflexivity, accountability, and co-creation in which ethical considerations involve everything from research design to engagement with consumers, diverse stakeholders, the public, and other academics, to taking insights and methods on from one project to develop for another. All these techniques are practiced in ways that are situated and contingent—they do not play out in the same way for every project. Rather, they are tailored to the situations and contingencies which emerge for the project at hand. With its focus on dynamic incipient moments at the crucible in which transformative change occurs, framed as "ethnographies of the possible" (Halse 2013) design anthropology represents a distinctive approach to future-making, characterized by its inclusive, collective, improvisational approach that seeks to transform its environment for the better.

HISTORY OF DESIGN

Industrial design, an early forerunner of modern design practice, started from the rise of the industrial revolution and the spread of mass marketing of consumer goods. The emergence of industrial design mirrored the growth of industrialization in Great Britain in the mid 18th century. As the industrial revolution expanded, labor was concentrated in factory work to increase production and efficiency, and former craft professions were dismantled. The design of products previously connected to production and personal selling of merchandise was divided into distinct roles. The designer, in manufacturing, created objects that were easy to produce and would appeal to consumer desires. Newly designed products emerged as potential sales tools for companies to convey their point of difference and employ fledgling marketing and advertising practices to imbue products symbolically with desire for consumers. Designers were the "new thing" to give companies a competitive advantage, especially during the hard times of the great depression in the late 1920s and 1930s.

Designers collaborated with management researchers and anthropologists to study worker productivity in industrial settings in the 1930s. The famous Hawthorne study showed how informal social processes of observing workers directly impacted the output and efficiency of factory workers. Other studies of industrial workers followed in the 1940s and 1950s, developing techniques for interaction analysis to predict elements of interpersonal behavior and create insights for business management. Industrial anthropologists were involved mainly in business management up until the Second World War, when new military fields of expertise developed that involved social scientists more extensively in product development through what was termed engineering psychology and human factors analysis (Reese 2002, 19–20).

Such studies mostly focused on the behavioral and psychological factors of workers, to gain control over the machinery, prevent accidents, and develop various new industrial products and equipment. Both in the United States and in Europe, where the influence from labor movements promoted concerns about workers' health and safety (Reese 2002, 20), research into engineering, human factors design, and behavior in the workplace led to social scientists' involvement in industrial design and business management. The field of design has only recently embraced ethnography as an integral part of design practice and theory worldwide. Anthropologists working as researchers since the late 1970s included ethnography and the importance of situating the product or service designed in a socio-cultural context of consumers' day lives as essential to understanding how products communicate use to users. In Europe, design anthropology developed from the participatory design movement that emerged in the 1970s in Scandinavia, when government and business partnered with designers to address complex social problems resulting from deindustrialization.

Participatory design involves users or stakeholders in the design and development of products, services, or systems. The goal of participatory design is to create solutions that better meet the needs of the users and are more usable and effective. Participatory design processes typically involve a series of workshops, interviews, and other forms of engagement with users. These activities may be led by designers, researchers, or facilitators, who are trained in participatory design methods. Participants may include end-users, clients, employees, and other stakeholders who have a stake in the success of the design. Participatory design has been used in a wide range of contexts, from designing software applications to urban planning. By involving users in the design process, participatory design is purported to create solutions that are more relevant, accessible, and useful to the people who will use them. It can also lead to greater buy-in and ownership of the final product or service, as users feel invested in its success.

The ethnographic approach incorporated into design in the US and Europe challenged the proliferation of design thinking based on cognitive psychology, made famous by Donald Norman (1988) who investigated cognitive design approaches, such as to discern whether to push or pull on a door to open it. Some door designs are notoriously confusing, but he opined that a flat bar extending horizontally across the midsection of a door affords no other operation but to push to open. This approach emphasizes product usability and human factors research in the study of design.

In contrast, ethnography has appealed to designers by revealing a whole new dimension of "the user" in social contexts. Ethnography investigates not only what consumers say they do, or what is in their mind, but what they actually do, and this may change by social context. This social context approach has uncovered discrepancies between intended social behavior and design, and actual social behavior. The merging of design and anthropology in the US occurred in contexts where business anthropologists have been engaged for decades in marketing and organizational research. In the 1980s, one of the first technology companies to bring in social scientists was Xerox PARC in Palo Alto, California, which hired a group of anthropologists led by Lucy Suchman, Jeanette Blomberg, and other colleagues. These anthropological researchers pioneered the use of ethnographic approaches in software design in the US.

At Xerox PARC, Suchman studied how people interact with machines in the workplace setting. In one example, computer scientists and engineers who had designed a new Xerox photocopier printer, assumed that office work was so straightforward and procedural that it should be tailor-made for computerization. The 8200 machine was outfitted with powerful new capabilities, such as automatic feeding and double-sided copying. But what Xerox had billed as a "self-evident" copier was proving a disaster in the real world of work. A video of the research showed office workers struggling to accomplish their copy job. Suchman suggested that instead of relying on the 8200's flashing error codes that had to be looked up in flip cards attached to the machine, a big green "start" button would greatly help. Ethnography reveals the underlying assumptions or tacit practices behind processes and products (especially ones in novel categories where conventions have not yet been established). Furthermore, skilled ethnographers go beyond observation to tailor their recommendations to specific contexts and business problems, delivering value not just for users, but for the company too.

Since the 1980s, ethnographic research has become an essential part of the interdisciplinary design and research communities of computer-supported cooperative work (CSCW) and human–computer interaction (HCI), where social scientists, computer scientists, and system designers shared knowledge about the use of technology in work practices (Wasson 2000, 380). Computer-supported cooperative work is the study of how people utilize technology collaboratively, often towards a shared goal. Human-centered design places people at the center of the development process to solve problems, enabling designers to create products and services that are tailored to the person. Research in these fields focused mainly on workplace settings of human–computer interaction and system design, with ethnography functioning as an essential component of gaining insights into the real-world experiences of users. Ethnomethodology drew attention to situated behavior and observable patterns to lead to theoretical insights about design.

In the 1990s, many firms embraced ethnography as essential to the design process and to business success. E-Lab, the Doblin Group, IDEO, and SonicRim applied ethnographic methods to industrial design and new product development. Ethnography became increasingly popular, so that, by the mid-1990s many companies in the US and Europe regularly employed anthropologists, as well as psychologists and sociologists, in projects that involved participant observation, video recording, qualitative interviews and analysis. The use of ethnography expanded beyond data gathering, as researchers saw its theoretical role in joining with design to reconfigure workspaces that challenged existing power relations in corporate settings. New developments, such as experience models and user profiles, helped to facilitate a shared analytical framework, along with uses of scenarios, user profiles, opportunity maps, and experience models, as interdisciplinary ways of bridging contrasts between understanding present practices and designing future ones.

Today, more than 90 design schools across the US train students in design pedagogy who can work at notable companies such as IDEO, Fitch, FrogDesign, among other firms. Communities such as Ethnographic Praxis in Industry Conference (EPIC) offers strong support for topics on design anthropology, and designers meet at Design Anthropological Futures conferences, the Participatory Design (PD) Conference, International Conference on Anthropology, Art and Design ICAAD, among others, as well as sites and communities such as AnthroDesign and Design History + Theory. These venues attest to the growing interest in design anthropology as a field for instigating and establishing lasting change for society.

ANTHROPOLOGY'S CRISIS OF REPRESENTATION: MATERIAL CULTURE AND DESIGN TO THE RESCUE

In 1986 the publication of *Writing Culture* along with several other books that critiqued anthropological intervention in the world hit the academic field of anthropology hard. James Clifford (1986, 9) called into question the entire anthropological process of fieldwork, author representations of others, and anthropological "write ups" that were purportedly "enmeshed in a world of enduring and changing power inequalities", and "enact (ing) power relations" limiting the representation of others. The critique questioned anthropological methods, concepts and even its object of study, culture.

Meanwhile, parallel to the "crisis of representation" in mainstream anthropology, alternative approaches in the form of material studies and, more recently, digital materiality and the investigation of the objective, offered a whole new theoretical way to engage the world. Arjun Appadurai's, *The Social Life of Things* (1986) and Bruno Latour and Steve Woolgar's, *Laboratory Life* (1986) focused on topics of materiality, non-human agency and the "built environment." These new assessments of culture helped decenter human representations and brought in new concepts that provided anthropology with an alternative trajectory for contributing to knowledge production. The rise of material culture, cultural material, and ecological approaches became legitimate subjects of analysis, which design anthropology embraced. Moving past the crisis of cultural representation and epistemological issues of "writing culture" that froze engagement in mainstream anthropology, the introduction of interventionist strategies in design anthropology along with new notions of the "agency of things" and the rise of "material studies," provided new paradigms for social action. This placed a new emphasis on, and enthusiasm for, the human capacity for change that was *intentional*. The new paradigm of design looks at the emergence of new forms of material agency and the ways in which people correspond (Ingold 2013) or interact with things so that humans are no longer the sole focus, but include their shared interactions with objects and the objective in creating and shaping their world.

The designed world and its material objects, along with human sociability, thus offers a rich and complex means for understanding cultures and societies. The premise holds that humans and their activities do not necessarily lie at the center of everything. Material culture offers an option, when combined with design studies, to avoid the problems of "othering" when investigating cultures. Material culture invites ethnographers to think about not only the status of things of "the other," but also to include their own material possessions in the interpretative process. It offers a way of overcoming the epistemological problems in writing culture. Growing interest in material culture and designing future possibilities also offers a way to perceive more idealistic understandings of culture and the practical conditions of human agency and its effect on climatic, environmental, and technical factors. The agency of things currently joins design thinking in ethnographic accounts to deal with actions of people and structures of societies, considering the specific role of material objects in helping to constitute both new actions, structures, and possible futures.

THE STUDY OF MATERIALITY

In our constructed world there is no longer a clear distinction between what is "design" and what is "culture." In everyday life, people commonly understand their normal environments as design, so design culture is no longer limited to professional studios and labs—it is out there, lived among people in daily life, from wearing an Apple Watch that can help keep the user healthy through biofeedback, to the organization of neighborhood parks, and helping to design nutritious meals served in a local school system. Design influences public perception and the social objectification of the designed work, when using various materials. Working with a design offers not one dimension of interpretation of the artist who designed it, but multiple and varied interpretations that are infused with social values, such as what does healthy food mean, or what should public park space include? The crucial role of material artifacts in the process of thinking is that the cognitive process should not be conceptualized as internal to a single individual, but instead be thought of as a social process that is shared in groups. The meaning of material agency emerges in the moment of social interaction so the objects that surround us can no longer be thought of as vessels of pre-existing meaning that can be decoded. Rather, material objects take a central role in cognition, and through continuous and repeated interactions with, and operations on, material objects, we make sense of the world. From the recursive and culturally shared nature of these interactions and operations, meaning is created and shared.

In looking at the influence of design on culture and its reciprocal, the impact of culture on design, we see how they are deeply entangled, complex, and often messy in formations and transformations of meanings, values, spaces, and the interactions they produce between people, objects, and histories. For example, designing for aging populations can focus on how older people interact with smartphones, such as avoiding clutter on screens, and designing for hand gestures that require only a single swipe; or designing for mobility can look at public bus networks and how people use them. This also must include anticipation and creation of new forms in ethnographic descriptions and theorizing to work with these populations.

TWO DESIGN AND MATERIALITY APPROACHES TO BUILDING BRIDGES

We can investigate the relation between production, materials used, the idea and consideration of a product and its design as it is created in a social context by comparing the social impact of the construction of two different bridges in the highlands of Borneo from two distinct approaches. One bridge is a traditional bamboo bridge that is built frequently by local villagers from intuitive design and embodied knowledge that is employed in the making. The other bridge is a concrete and wire cable suspension bridge that starts out with a preordained design drawn on paper, and yet was modified in context due to unforeseen circumstances.

Ian Ewart (2013) writes an informative ethnography about these two approaches to bridge making and the intersection between engineering, materiality, and actuation. His two contrastive examples detail the issues relevant to design anthropologists: what is the practice of actually making something? In both cases of bridge development, design happens as part of production, in the making, rather than as a separate stage that is prior to the process of making the bridge. The point Ewart wishes to make is that designed objects are created socially as well as materially in context, and this becomes evident as he explores the processes involved in two bridge designs and their executions.

Ewart informs us that a bridge was needed for the community in the Kelabit highlands of Borneo, since the old one washed away in a flood in 2008. Local villagers set out to build a bamboo bridge, as they had done for generations, with existing local materials and traditional cultural knowledge. Bamboo bridges are essentially a series of poles anchored on each bank and raised to meet over the center of the river. The poles are bound together with rattan to form a shallow arch. The design of the bridge means that it flexes and bounces as people transverse it. The whole structure is strengthened by rattan stringers tied to overhead trees. Nevertheless, while these materials are easily accessed and local, they are also perishable, so while bamboo bridges are rapid to assemble, they need frequent repairs or rebuilding after a year or two, especially after periods of heavy rain.

Then, in 2010, the thought was to make a more permanent bridge that would stand up to weather and change. A second bridge was planned for the local area but this time with a more permanent solution mandated from foreign developments that arrived in the area to take charge of the project. Suspension bridges are far sturdier, made of tall support towers, large concrete anchor blocks with posts, cable wire ropes and a wooden walkway. This design was introduced by British troops stationed in the area in the 1960s. Yet, for the locals making the bridge, the details were vaguely understood, shaped by sparse knowledge of other hanging suspension bridges. The process took much longer but resulted in a more permanent bridge. Lack of details meant that decisions, mistakes, and new discoveries were made during the construction.

How do we compare production or "design" processes of an intuitive, informally created bridge with an unfamiliar, innovative new style bridge? The first bridge was traditional and followed a similar procedure known through generations of making bamboo bridges; the second bridge was built according to a more formal design, using new materials that were innovative but unfamiliar. Socially among villagers, the traditional bridge generated very little discussion or trouble, while the new, unfamiliar bridge required a detailed plan that remained incomplete. In design, raw materials exist in relation to their environment and the designer intercedes to change the potential form of some of the parts. The environment, then, is relational and responsible for the process of making, beyond the intent of the person involved. The person and his/her actions are directed and informed by the materials as well as directing and forming them. This mutual confluence of person, materials, and environment in the process of making also recognizes that the conceptual design is never perfectly actualized but formed in the making as a response to circumstances. Design, such as in engineering, must recognize that the skills of production are also part of design. This is best exemplified by the two bridge constructions that took on different social and cultural dynamics as materials and sociality shaped their interactions.

In the end, both bridges served their functional purposes, but their processes drew on different forms of social making and from different forms of materiality. It shows that design and production are not separate activities and neither is design an act of pre-conception, but designing and making are entangled in a complex relationship of doing. Design happens "on the go, in the hand" (Ewart 2013, 98) as an iterative process and as part of the performance of making. Understanding materiality and social context can help anthropologists mitigate social tensions and work towards better integration of design with desired social situations.

For design anthropologists, the lesson learned is that materiality means not only taking the material world as a focus for ethnographic conversations, but also integrating the cultural frameworks through which people understand those material worlds. Better explanation and earlier involvement with local villagers would have helped in developing the second bridge. Design research commonly explores the material spaces and things around users in this way. Design anthropologists do more than understand "situated practices" (Suchman 2011) of people in a context to maximize product efficiency; they do *knowledge work*, which is heuristic, producing collaborative, best-fit scenarios that tap into ecosystems of design knowledge and sociality, and which extend far beyond professional sites to create real change in people's lives.

DESIGNING SOCIAL CHANGE: SERVICE DESIGN

In the realm of consumption, services are a different kind of consumer offering than tangible products. Services consist of activities, benefits, or satisfactions that are essentially intangible and do not result in the ownership of anything but are derived instead solely from experience. Services provide customers with a transformational experience: from dirty to clean (cleaning services), from ignorant to informed (educational services), from sick to healthy (healthcare services). Services are ephemeral in that they only exist during their consumption when the skill and expertise of the service provider (e.g., hair stylist) are applied to the customer to achieve a transformation and produce an outcome. As such, services are co-produced through collaborations and interactions between providers of the service and consumers who receive it. The value of the service is, therefore, dependent on the particular relationship between service provider and consumer.

The service industry influence is enormous and growing, consisting of 80% of the business field in the US. Services range from the proliferation of low-end service jobs, such as DoorDash or Grubhub food delivery services, to higher end professional services, such as financial, healthcare, retail, hotel, airline travel, and government services, among others. In addition, new kinds of digitally enhanced services and service relationships are shaping the service worlds. For example, algorithms on Netflix help predict what viewers enjoy and make recommendations for new programs based on viewing characteristics. Clearly, an economy fueled by services is changing the socio-material conditions in which we live, as services are integrated into the fabric of everyday life.

Service design is a process and discipline that involves designing and improving the experience of these services, from the customer's perspective. Service design can be applied to improve existing services or to create new services and can be used to design both physical and digital services. Service design is not the design of everything. It is a specialization, just as are graphic design, industrial design, interaction design, UX, and customer experience design.

Designing a service might include working on beginning-to-end dimensions of an entire service or designing for a service moment. Within that service, there are environments, systems, people, and tools. Service design, in this sense, takes a holistic approach to service delivery, considering all aspects of the service experience, including the physical and digital touchpoints, the interactions between customers and service providers, and the overall service system. The design process starts with understanding the intent, and what things need to be achieved in support of the service, sometimes working together with the designer or engineer to make a cohesive whole. It also involves a deep understanding of customer behavior and expectations, the entire journey that a consumer experiences, as well as the organization's goals and objectives.

Service design methods often involve co-creation and collaboration with stakeholders, such as customers, employees, and partners. This helps to ensure that the service is designed with the customer's perspective in mind and meets their needs. Thus, we can see that the increase in services will continue to alter social arrangements, and the intentional and unintentional consequences are fertile grounds for anthropologists to investigate.

When designing services, we must consider that, increasingly, recipients are also co-producers and co-creators of value. For instance, the rise of the "sharing economy" sees services enacted peer-to-peer through technology enabled networks of people, bypassing the traditional service provider and empowering consumers directly. Examples of co-created/co-produced services include Airbnb, which allows individuals to offer spare rooms in their homes to other customers, or blending domestic and professional services, such as when ordinary people become Uber drivers to take on a second income (Blomberg and Darrah 2015). In these examples, the actions of recipients affect service outcomes and the attending value received by both provider and recipient. People must learn how to participate in service encounters by identifying and ascribing meaning and value to elements in the service, asking, for instance, what makes for a good home stay or car ride?

DESIGNING CUSTOMER EXPERIENCE JOURNEYS

Designing services that deliver high-quality, human-centered experiences have always been an important part of creating value for companies. Disney has long manufactured dreams and memories through its entertaining movies and destination theme parks.

It carefully plans every stage and interaction of consumer experience in relation to Disney properties. The goal of service design is to create services that are easy to use, accessible, and meet the needs and expectations of the customer. Moreover, the main takeaway of a service experience is that it is memorable, so users are likely to repeat the service.

A central challenge for service designers, then, is objectifying the design of the service into steps of an experience journey. Journeys are made tangible through interactions or "touch points" between people and between people and things, and through such encounters between service providers and recipients, services are realized. Therefore, designing a service journey involves adjusting and modifying the performance of various touch point engagements along the experience journey of the service, and counting on some sort of transformation to occur as a result. Designing a service, then, designs for outcomes in the transformation that designers hope to achieve. This also suggests a strategy of working backwards from outcomes to consider each step or lever along the way. What are the affordances that allow for the right conditions for maximal interactions and relationships to happen?

Describing service journeys ethnographically is the first step in designing more complex services and ultimately introducing greater predictability in service outcomes. For example, I worked on a project to re-imagine Ruth's Chris Steakhouse in terms of redesigning the consumer experience journey. Our objective was to design a future vision of a customer experience that would inspire and empower the organization to deliver on Ruth's Chris brand promise in the context of current and future customer needs and behaviors.

REDESIGNING THE STEAKHOUSE EXPERIENCE

We conducted ethnographic research in 2013 among users of steakhouses in three markets: Los Angeles, Chicago, and Orlando. From a marketing perspective, we sought to understand what made Ruth's Chris unique and distinctive in positioning against its competitors. From a design perspective, we explored end-user touch points of interaction to improve the overall experience.

Before mapping out the experience journey, we interviewed respondents and reported their recollections of steakhouse experiences: "Ruth's Chris, it's okay. Nothing bad, nothing good. Service isn't bad either, it's okay—I keep using the word 'okay'—because that's all it is." "I like Ruth's Chris, Morton's, and Gibson's. They're all pretty similar. None of them are head and shoulders above the other." Or "Seems like steakhouses are created equal and there's nothing to push me over the edge to go there." From our investigation into the service experience, many steakhouses offer interesting and new elements, but none are offering a better experience that sets any brand apart.

Then we introduced the concept of ritual to differentiate and distinguish Ruth's Chris from competitors, since ritual experiences exist on emotional, physical, intellectual, social, and spiritual levels. Our research suggested that the more experiential and sensory realms of the steakhouse ritual that we might tap into, the more powerful the experiential effect and lasting the memory for the user. The client and our team agreed to engage a multisensory experience in the user journey and to anchor it in ritual to make the Ruth's Chris experience more transformative and memorable in outcome.

Steakhouse dining is ritualistic for a number of reasons: steak is a primal and carnal food (sacred in sacrifices, taboo in other cultures); taking a guest (spouse, partner, client, relative) to a steakhouse signals a special relationship with that person; steakhouses have a protocol in service, the formality is elaborate and part of the specialness of the journey; food and drink at steakhouses are not delicate and decorative but substantial and indulgent. As respondents said, the food is "real and honest." Time seems to slow down, conversations matter more, care and intimacy is expressed.

Moreover, understanding the steakhouse dining experience as a ritual provided us with a useful theoretical framework in which to interpret observations, discussions, actions of waiters, the specialness of the setting, and how these cues imbue the experience as unique. Victor Turner in *The Ritual Process* (1969) builds upon van Gennep's observation that rituals are liminal in that they temporarily extricate participants from their social statuses. Rites of passage are also antithetical to existing social structure and create a "subjunctive" mood, where they invite a space for transformation and new possibilities. This ritual framework helped us understand how the steakhouse experience needed to be further set apart from daily routines for guests, follow an ordered sequence of steps, recognize a special space where normal rules are suspended, allow for emotional satisfaction of guests, and ultimately be recurring, so guests would wish to return.

We broke down the steakhouse ritual dining experience into five touch points or stages: anticipation; arrival; immersion; transformation; reflection. First, anticipation was designed around the choice of the restaurant. This is when user expectations are highest and includes making a reservation at the restaurant and driving to the location. The build-up of excitement and anxiety for the expected steakhouse presets the anticipation experience. Our designed restaurant response to the anticipation stage is for restaurant management to ask guests about the type of occasion when the reservation is made and prepare for the guests arrival.

The stage of arrival follows with valet parking, entering the restaurant and informing the host/hostess of your arrival. Arrival designed properly means the restaurant helps in transitioning guests from shedding reality and decompressing to slowing down and opening the mind to the meal ahead.

Following arrival comes the stage of immersion. This is where the service of restaurant staff, the material quality of food served, the ambiance, noise and scents create for guests a sense of separation and escapism. As one guest mentioned, "Entering the restaurant begins my mini vacation." As a table or booth is offered and guests sit down, interaction with the waiter, drinks, appetizers, and ordered meals begins the transformation to a secluded realm of entertainment, engagement, and the guests' absorption with each other in a special space.

Following this touch point, the transformation crescendos. The restaurant helps transition guests by creating a zone to move from the outside world into the steakhouse experience. Guests are treated to indulgent pleasures, enjoying an elaborate meal, where everything is as they desire: no rules, only indulgences. Designing the ultimate transformative service means orchestrating a rhythm to service, matching the flow of service to match the guest's dining experience. Transformation proceeds, with sensory fulfillment and a change in mindset, because of the immersion that inspires the unfolding of the ritual. The transformative journey results in the guest feeling taken care of and is left feeling enthusiastic about a return visit.

Reflection is the final stage in the journey, where the restaurant can acknowledge the guest's visit in hopes of establishing a lasting connection. Reflection involves consideration, evaluation and savoring of the steakhouse experience. The restaurant can enhance the reflective experience by providing a memorable ending to the guest's experience with delightful keepsakes—such as cookies to go, or a doggy bag treat for the pet waiting at home. Customers can reflect on returning to Ruth's Chris for consistency and dependable expectations in food, service and atmosphere.

Our project blended this ritual breakdown into a convergent duality of service design and experience journey mapping, since service design is both strategic and tactical. We implemented these changes to redesign the service experience at Ruth's Chris steakhouse, to match and exceed the heightened expectations of customer experience. Service design can thus be a prolonged act of designing harmony between people and the organization when it is broken down into meaningful units so that each touch point is maximized for user satisfaction. Insights into the flow of service helped the organization imagine a future where their service can be transformational and bring the consumer experience to life.

DESIGN FICTION FOR EMERGENT TECHNOLOGIES AND DESIGNING FUTURES

Design ethnography can also be applied to imaginary scenarios, or fictive studies, of designing the future. In these scenarios, design anthropologists are faced with challenges of emerging or even non-existent technologies, where the future market is much less defined. A technology is considered as "emerging" when it causes a radical change to business, industry, or society. Because its primary impact occurs in the future, an emerging technology is marked by ambiguity as well as by uncertainty on ROI and penetration rate. The emergent technology does not need to be a new invention—it can also be a reapplication of an existing technology in a new domain. Companies that build emerging technology products face a unique challenge, namely that, by definition, the market for these products is largely undefined. I discuss ethnographies of contemporary sci-fi movies as one means to imagine future scenarios for design planning. Since the product may not exist, it creates additional challenges for research.

Design ethnography's ability to transform situated observation into understanding of the near future, while also being anchored in the present, is key to formulating anticipatory ethnography of far-off futures. Speculative design strives to open a discursive space that is underwritten by the unavoidable plurality of the future. The idea is not to show how things will be, but, rather, to open up a space for discussion of what things could be, in the present. Creating a believable and relatable story world allows design fictions to first represent, and then explore, the nuances and mundanity of future circumstances.

A healthy design fiction situates the viewer in a prospective future so they can envision it in a meaningful way. Designers create not material but "*diegetic*" prototypes or story prototypes that act to suspend disbelief in the future. Prototyping is a key part of many design processes, often employed by designers as an internal stimuli or shorthand to a project, allowing designers to play with ideas before committing to one. It is a powerful tool that allows designers and design teams to understand how the mocked-up product might manifest itself in experimental ways in a finished product.

In the concept of designing the future through stories, the diegesis prototype is the "world of the story."

Virtually all design constraints are removed, and the diegetic prototype can transcend the time horizon of the present and arrive at a compelling future, free from temporal constraints. Diegetic prototyping through storytelling is not new; such prototypes exist within DaVinci's inventions, in works of fiction from Jules Verne's *The Time Machine*, in comic book series such as Stan Lee's *X-men*, and television series such as *Star Trek*. In almost any science fiction work some form of story prototype exists. What designers seek to understand with these possible futures, is how they can be normalized in current society, and place social norms within them to test out futures and technologies; in such ways, *Star Trek* communicators conceived in the 1960s as a possible future technology are actualized in today's mobile phones.

DIALOGUES WITH THE FUTURE

The authors Joseph Lindley, Dhruv Sharma, and Robert Potts (2014) suggest looking at design fiction prototypes through the analysis of process, audience, and content: three approaches in anticipatory ethnography. First, they study the process of creating a design fiction; studying how creators, directors, and actors come up with ideas and normalize them in stories; then they investigate how the designated audiences interact with, or perceive, a design fiction; and finally, they study the actual content of a design fiction for social feasibility. For example, these three elements help evaluate designing a future and building a story prototype that can be evidenced in the 2013 film *Her*, directed by Spike Jonze. *Her* represents a Hollywood fictive movie that blends a future sci-fi drama with everyday romance—the protagonist, Joaquin Phoenix, falls in love with his phone's operating system which has advanced AI capabilities and leads him on. The value of understanding the romance between Joaquin Phoenix and the operating system, portrayed by the voice of Scarlett Johansson, is valuable to predicting the future ways consumers increasingly interact with intelligent machine learning, AI, and other forms of advanced machine thinking that are rapidly transforming society today. How do you normalize AI in society? You craft a personal story of a human falling in love with it.

Studying the process of creating the film fiction, Spike Jonze purportedly realized while producing the film that "[*Her*] isn't a movie about technology. It's a movie about people" (Vanhemert, 2014), hinting at Jonze's "interior" relationship with the narrative of the film. The process also shows how the actors embraced the script, relating to AI as if a real person in a real relationship. The design ethnographers then study how audiences interact with, or perceive, the design fiction. This supposition pivots around the strength of the narrative; it must be believable and relatable to the individual realities of the audience. Referring to *Her*, the production team went to considerable lengths to make the fictional future depicted in the film appear familiar, even mundane. The apartments in which human characters live look ordinary enough, they eat meals that look normal, drink coffee and socialize, as would any ordinary person. The technological future is made ordinary to fit and embed in the story so that the audience is, it is hoped, absorbed into the future.

Next, studying the content of a design fiction—film reviews of *Her* exemplify the richness of the film's story and appear to contain insights that parallel what the ethnographers find. In this mode, critics, reviewers, and ethnographers arrive at similar conclusions, accepting and realizing the potential of the film in predicting and actualizing the fiction, such that they are "narratively situated" and the story of the future becomes immediately relevant in the present.

Projecting possible futures of design through such fictional narratives is essential for confronting the pace of change in the 21st century, along with the increasingly vivid notions of "future shock" and "wicked problems." Casting such fictional narratives creates new ways of understanding, preparing for, and even pre-empting the future that is more compelling than ever. The vastness of the problem space that humans are encountering requires a suitably bold response. Anticipatory ethnography and design futures takes a response and sees how visions can become a reality. Design fiction and design ethnography communities will further join to develop these ideas, extend the concept, and demonstrate the merits, shortcomings, relevance, and scope of this work, through empirical investigations.

CONCLUSION

This chapter has intended to inform readers about the variety of approaches and uses of design anthropology and explore the many ways it offers a distinct style of knowledge. Beyond its early days of offering ethnographically informed design, where ethnography merely added a research dimension to design, design anthropology today has come to represent a distinctive approach to future-making, characterized by inclusive, collaborative, and public approaches to design that focus on dynamic situations and social relationships. Rather than see design as only the creation of objects, design anthropology incorporates improvisation and social situations in everyday life, where people create new realities and transform their social environments.

Design anthropology has emerged and distinguished itself from traditional anthropology, especially in how it has borrowed generously from anthropology's main methodology, ethnography, and theories. We might ask the inverse, how could a revised academic anthropology benefit from design anthropology? By drawing on the similarities and correspondences they both share in ethnography, Keith Murphy and George Marcus (2013), suggest the following: if design ethnography could be reduced to an essence or an entity, it would be its capability of transforming raw information about something into "useful knowledge," taking mere ideas and "cooking" them into delectable concepts. In this way, a feasible design becomes objectified and put to *purposeful use* in the world. Design ethnography does this by following a process involving ideas, research, reflexivity, and specific goals in the service of benefiting people. Its actions consist of techniques and methods that "work with" and "work through" different kinds of materials. As a reflexive and iterative process, it is always moving back and forth between thought and action, adjusting for best fit, and not always seeking ideal outcomes but allowing for creativity and new concepts to emerge. In this way, say Murphy and Marcus, academic anthropology could "benefit from the ways designers handle their material and the creativity they bring to their work" (2013, 262). In other words, academic anthropology could learn to commit to creative and thoughtful ways to instigate positive change in the world.

NOTE

1 Some argue that design anthropology is a distinct field from business anthropology.

A DIGITAL ANTHROPOLOGY APPROACH TO CULTURE

The rise of the digital world has challenged the field of traditional anthropology, offering new careers for business anthropologists by introducing new field sites and new methods for understanding the complexity of human activity. Beyond investigating technological devices and digital programs, such as smartphones, social media apps, or computer software, for their engineering or design functions, anthropologists seek to understand the *meaning* of these digital objects and subjects in people's everyday lives and how they instigate social change. We are at an inflection point, where global efforts need to address broad social problems such as online misinformation, political divides and the rise of hate groups, and the precarious balance between care and surveillance in our human populated sites. Anthropology can uniquely address these problems because it offers holistic, reflexive, and empathetic solutions. Digital innovators in anthropology are finding ways to create, design and work with new technologies and offer digital methodologies to help address issues such as gender, racial and social inequalities by using artificial intelligence (AI), machine learning (ML), big data, computer algorithms and data science[1] in their work.

This chapter examines recent trends of innovative anthropologists in their work of addressing these social issues, as they forecast new directions for society by promoting online art communities, stopping hate groups, or exploring the current and future effects of telepresence or teleoperated robots, drones, and self-driving autonomous cars. Digital anthropology offers an exciting new field of academic scholarship and social practice for anthropologists to address the ways in which the digital, material,[2] and social worlds are entangled in

DOI: 10.4324/9781003358930-6

processes and products that impact society. Moreover, ethnographic methods in digital technologies and collaboration with other data scientists in research opens the way for anthropologists to attend to current social concerns as well as future-oriented challenges that new technologies present. Anthropological theories and methodologies can, importantly, bring innovation to digital tools and processes in order to uncover deep human insights into global and local communities. Doing so will enable a global effort for more ethical and inclusive societies. Anthropologists are, thus, helping to understand and direct these challenges that new technologies and digital futures bring, as they investigate digital technology in the communities, society, and the world we live in.

WHY STUDY DIGITAL CULTURE? DIGITAL ANTHROPOLOGY IN THE EVERYDAY LIFE OF MEDIA ECOLOGIES

With the growth of social media, AI, big data, data analytics, and other technologically mediated forms of communication and social interaction, the digital is being incorporated into all aspects of daily life. The distinction between online and offline worlds is less relevant since activities in both realms become blended and merged in our society: the two spaces interact with and transform each other. The internet in particular, and the digital world in general, represent, not a radical break from past traditions of culture investigation and neither do they usher in a whole new world of human expression, communication, and consumption. Rather, as Daniel Miller and Heather Horst (2012) and Haidy Geismar and Hannah Knox (2021) assert, the digital world blends and interacts with the material and social world of users, which reflect broader social and cultural worlds and identities, and offers the means for anthropologists to better understand changes and adaptations to people's lives.

An earlier point made by Miller and Horst (2012) about the relevance of studying the digital world holds true: that anthropology is still the science of humanity and its traditional commitment to holism still applies to digital studies. This means no person lives an entirely digital life. Evidence of holism is evident in the fact that all media, whether reading books, watching television, or visiting friends on Instagram on our smartphones, are part of a wider "media ecology" with interdependent relationships. Hence, it is not easy to treat each new media separately, but rather consider the idea that media integrate, build off one another, and not only strongly influence us, but are likely the primary cause of social change. The speed at which new media are accepted and become normalized contrasts and compares with how quickly other "new" media become old. For instance, "old" media technology platforms such as Facebook have declined 1.5% in user growth in 2022, while new social media, such as TikTok, have grown in advertising revenue from $8 billion in 2016, to $38.6 billion in 2021. TikTok is the most popular social media app among youth 4–15 years old, with 44% of global youth, spending an average use time of 75 minutes per day (Qustodio 2022).

Digital anthropologists also investigate how digital culture plays a widespread social role today, affecting consumer attitudes, market trends, and audience preferences. For instance, understanding the dynamics of online communities can inform strategies for online marketing campaigns, customer engagement with brands, and brand communities in the digital environment. Similarly, examining digital media can inform business practices related to applied semiotics and marketing within a digital context. Furthermore, understanding digital behavior is crucial to UX and product development, with significant implications for the future competitiveness of organizations. Companies struggle to remain relevant in a business landscape increasingly dominated by software that can detect emerging patterns and trends and provide actionable recommendations for marketing, product development, or customer service enhancements. Anthropologists working for these companies can assist them in developing competitive strategies by making the most of AI, digital tools, and other technologies that help understand consumer behavior.

ANTHROPOLOGISTS INVESTIGATE THE DIGITAL WORLD FROM ONLINE COMMUNITIES AND VIRTUAL WORLDS TO BIG DATA

Anthropological investigations of the digital world are recent and have rapidly expanded over the last few years. Early researchers focused on the digital as a social subject, apart from other cultural activities. Christine Hine's (2000) *Virtual Ethnography* was prompted by the rise of online communities, as her study sought to understand what constituted "net life." Other scholars focused on online sites of social interaction, looking more deeply into how people experienced their lives in the virtual worlds they created. Bonnie Nardi's (2010) exploration of the *World of Warcraft* and Tom Boellstorff's (2015) examination of *Second Life* investigated the lives of its members and what constituted social interactions and cultures that formed within these virtual worlds. Still other studies focused on the digital extension of data collection as a research tool and the rapid rise of big data and data analytics. Techniques such as "Ethnomining" and Geiger and Ribes's (2011) "Trace ethnography" examined organic sources of data from users to create a more holistic picture of users' lives. Robert Kozinets (2009) developed an online web-based ethnography called Netnography for the investigation of online brand communities. Microsoft anthropologists and researchers, dana boyd and Kate Crawford (2012), implored anthropologists and data analysts to apply a humanistic sensitivity to rising big data studies, alerting us to the human patterns that big data reveal. Big data is impressive, they maintain, not for their size or speed of facts gathered, but for revealing actual socialities, subjectivities, and social practices of people under investigation.

Anthropologists in business have noted that big data analytics provides powerful consumer and end-user insights on a broader scale than single site ethnography can. Large consumer organizations have gathered vast amounts of data with sophisticated programs to search for human insights that improve their marketing of products and services to their consumers, based on personal and social characteristics. For instance, Tesco, a large UK retailer, collected huge amounts of data on its customers' shopping habits that allowed it to send precisely targeted coupons. Noting that when a household couple started buying diapers, signaling the arrival of a new baby, Tesco would send discount vouchers for beer to the household, knowing that the new father would have less of an opportunity to go to the pub (*The Economist* 2012).

In another example, John Curran (2013) discusses how big data provides the ability to tap into consumers' desires in ways that may be unconscious to them. He discusses how big data algorithms can track people's discourses of excitement or utopia in social media to make the world a better place for us. He cites an article by Jane Wakefield, technology reporter at the BBC, where she explores how big data is used to understand what makes cities "happy" or "unhappy". Wakefield notes that research carried out by the Advanced Computing Center at the University of Vermont used 37 million geolocated tweets from 180,000 people in the US to explore the "happiness" factor in specific locations where people lived. They found that words such as "starving" and "heartburn" were more often used in tweets within cities with high rates of obesity. However, the key point of this type of research was to monitor in real-time the exchanges of people to indicate changing moods and behaviors in urban populations (Wakefield 2013, cited in Curran 2013).

GROWTH OF AI, MACHINE LEARNING, AND DATA SCIENCE

The current wave of anthropologists is immersed in digitalization, AI, and the deep learning of neural networks as they explore what it means to be human and how AI influences social relations. Humans and technology are now inextricably linked in a dynamic and reciprocal relationship, and even technically now machines are also caught in a "loop" with other machines, or "themselves," which remains unpredictable in outcome. Reframing previous studies of what it means for humans to grow up, have friends and develop an identity in virtual worlds of *Second Life* or *World of Warcraft*, anthropologists might currently ask, how can we understand to "see the world like an artificial intelligence that has been raised in a specific data world?" (Munk 2023, 30). Anthropologists are beginning to apply their theories and methods to assist in understanding and shaping emerging new digital worlds. Innovative approaches discussed in this chapter show an expanding field of digital studies, with new added technologies that are more capable, influential, and pervasive in our lives, especially regarding what the digital might bring to our futures.

A new area for digital anthropologists to explore involves the intersection of human inquiry, cultural analysis, and the rising use of AI, machine learning, and algorithms in programming. This comes at a time when the rapid digitalization of our world is changing areas of business practice, commerce, consumer marketing and consumption, media and communications, and design studies.

Business anthropologists are studying and working with emerging digital technologies (Artz, 2023; Hillier, 2023; Koycheva, 2023; Lanzeni, et al., 2023; Pink, 2022), trying to assess their impact—specifically in the field of AI—as a substantial societal disruption and opportunity for business, as well as for new anthropological research. Anthropologists and data scientists are collaborating to understand rapid social changes as they occur. While new technologies such as AI, immersive realities, and the widespread prevalence of social media permeate people's lives, these new social phenomena also become embedded in society and everyday life as dimensions of culture, and further create cultural expressions when elements become normalized in the lived and shared experiences of people.

For instance, emoji language and newer characters on smartphones and on apps continue to expand the ways humans communicate and express themselves digitally. In April 2020, Facebook introduced a new "Care" emoji depicting hugging a heart amid the COVID-19 pandemic. But this action in social media also raises questions for anthropologists of what it means to express care for others in a digital space and especially in a time of loss and mourning (see Proctor and Adely 2021). Digital anthropologists are working with data scientists to develop interdisciplinary methods, tools, and theories to help better understand changes in culture and bring the cultural context of anthropology to scale in solving social problems.

ADDRESSING SOCIAL ISSUES DIGITALLY

Some of the global challenges anthropologists face are dealing with the spread of hate groups, misinformation, the rise of social and political polarization, the mental health crisis, the expansion of digital surveillance, and growing digital inequalities. Effective research depends on anthropologists' ability to gain deeper insights into the relationship between people and digital technologies, and to see and understand people, cultures, and communities online.

For instance, Katie Hillier (2023) discusses the intersection of anthropology and data science and how an anthropologist working with the Brazilian government helps track and understand extremist social movements. Hillier details the work of Leticia Cesarino, a digital anthropologist employed at the federal University of Santa Catarina (USFC) in Brazil. Cesarino works collaboratively with data scientists to track threats and election fraud by blending digital anthropology with data science to understand the online behaviors of far-right radical groups on the social media app, Telegram. She helps develop algorithms that work in conjunction with traditional ethnographic approaches. Previously, her ethnographic work missed higher up and broader "systems-level perspectives," on how various groups spread disinformation and how people came together for rallies. She needed to "see how algorithms could add to the conventional ethnographic outlook by showing an ecosystem view from the outside to identify systemic patterns across various users, influencers and algorithms" (2023, 4). While the algorithmic platform is designed by data scientists, Cesarino creates the search queries that specify cultural context and language meaning. She gathers this data from real-time ethnographic immersions among various communities, which otherwise would remain invisible in data searches. By combining machine learning with humanistic perspectives on group behavior, she helps identify problems and predict when far right extremists might rally an attack, as happened in Brazil when a group of Jair Bolsonaro supporters stormed the government buildings against the democratically elected president, Lula da Silva. As Cesarino's work demonstrates the usefulness of applying digital methods to traditional ethnographic approaches, the question remains: how can the use of AI gain broader acceptance among other anthropologists and help them in their work across a variety of fields?

HOW THE USE OF AI CAN ENHANCE AND IMPROVE HUMAN ETHNOGRAPHIC TECHNIQUES

Traditional ethnographic methods in anthropology have shown their limitations, especially in cross-cultural research. The issue of ethnographic limitations brought about a "crisis" of representation in anthropology in the 1970s and1980s. Scholars[3] questioned the traditional approach to fieldwork, in the lone researcher venturing out to study, write about and represent "her" or "his" culture. James Clifford (1986, 7) faulted the lone anthropologist's ability to adequately represent other people, reinforcing the "theorizing about the limits of representation itself." Written cultural accounts, he claimed, represent only "partial truths" because ethnography itself was "incomplete."

In response, solutions were proposed to address these shortcomings, notably by George Marcus (1995), who proposed multi-sited ethnography and collaborative work with others. He invited multidisciplinary work with media studies, science, and technology to help shape anthropological research, bridge dichotomies of local and global, and follow the circulation of "cultural meanings, objects and identities" (1995, 96) across time and space. What was needed, he posited, was a "mobile ethnography" (1995, 49) that could map out and trace cultural formations across and within multiple sites of activity, reducing unhelpful distinctions and problems of an overly localized perspective from singular ethnographic accounts.

Notably, much of what Marcus called for to improve ethnography back in the mid 1990s, is answered today in using AI combined with ethnography. AI solves many issues that individual anthropologists alone cannot address. Ethnography with AI is collaborative, joining anthropologists with other data scientists, designers, urban planners, and AI itself. Ethnography and AI can grow and extend rapidly to other sites; they can "follow the circulation of cultural meanings, objects and identities" across time and space, where multi-sited ethnography is aided by sensors in multiple locations, scales operations across many sites, and can employ robots to help assess contextual data. Moreover, if anthropologists working with data scientists can program algorithms with the latest concepts and ideas from anthropological theory, AI could help pick up and supplement what the human anthropologist misses in sensory studies, gender equality, power relations, forms of speaking (discourses), metaphor analysis, practice theory, and so forth. One anthropologist may not have all this knowledge available to apply to a study, but an AI assisted algorithm might.

AI allows anthropologists to study a community and rapidly scale the inquiry to larger data sets across multiple locations. In this way, AI can achieve similar access to, and greater collections of inconsistencies in, "What people say, what people do, and what they say they do (as) entirely different things"" (Margaret Mead's famous dictum, quoted in Miles 2000, 13) at greater scale, since AI can triangulate data points.

For example, Lora Koycheva (2023), in a more radical article, proposes that future anthropological research will ultimately use AI equipped teleoperated robots to help ethnographers sense a local context through embodied processes. A team effort between robotics engineers and anthropologists or ethnographers will send AI assisted robots, fitted with sensors and AI thinking, to multiple sites to conduct research. Robots in locations will be able to scale a sense of placement, embodiment, and contextual presence at a speed and scale, allowing the human behind the machine to stay connected in far-off environments. Robots will be able to transport a person's senses, presence, and abilities to act on and manipulate the physical environment at a distance, such as "give a hug, or pick up an object – at a remote location in real time" (2023, 1). Although in early stages of development, the telepresence robotic avatar systems enable humans to "transport" their embodied presence to remote situations. Humanoid avatar systems (robots) with torsos and limbs would allow the anthropologist a life-like presence in remote locations, using the full range of their senses in real time through an action–perception feedback loop. By being "physically present" in a remote location, the anthropologist can control their remote body, act through it at that remote location, as well as receive physical feedback from the events there, thus allowing the anthropologist to be able to manipulate and control the humanoid robot at a great distance. Koycheva writes that the usefulness of such robotic researchers would extend into dangerous situations for humans where research is needed, such as employing teleoperated ethnography in a world in which lockdowns occur due to pathogens, or in tense areas of border closures due to conflict, or for environmental disasters. In this way, anthropologists innovate and improve ethnographic techniques, not only with their theories and methods, but also potentially with enhanced robotic bodies.

The business world depends heavily on economics and data science when it comes to understanding digital impacts, but these sciences alone don't tell the whole story. Economic models for big data are built for scale, but struggle with providing insightful depth. These models can describe in quantitative methods the "what" and "when" of human behavior, but not answer the more intriguing "how" and "why." Furthermore, experience shows us that over-reliance on one-dimensional approaches magnifies social biases and ethical blind spots. This is where digital anthropologists focus on the intersection between technology and humans, examining the quantitative and qualitative elements, using big data and thick data, the virtual and real, to understand consumer trends. Data science with ethnography needs greater investment by anthropologists and public awareness of its unique and untapped potential to humanize decision-making for leaders across the public and private sectors. Anthropologists may ask, how do human communities and societies interact and are shaped by technologies and, accordingly, how can policies be rendered more ethical and inclusive?

DEVELOPING AN ANTHROPOLOGY OF COMPUTER LEARNING

What if the next generation of anthropologists were to write computer algorithms to model or even explain culture? Many academic anthropologists are clearly against any formalist or quantitative forms of cultural analysis. They believe it runs counter to proper ethnographic interpretation, involving in-person, in-context cultural analysis, or thick description, as Geertz imagined (Munk et al. 2022). Yet, questions for today's new digital age are: what are we missing if we don't engage digital life as the world does; what if computers could aid in ethnographic fieldwork; what if they can describe and detail consumer behavior through algorithmic sensemaking as well or better than their human colleagues?

If we take the interpretative approach of Geertz and apply it to machine learning, could we change academic resistance to digital efforts in ethnography? Digital anthropologists (Artz 2023, Seaver 2018, Munk et al. 2022; Paff (2021) ask this very question and suggest that AI can successfully contribute to interpreting cultural expressions equally well or even better than traditional human conducted ethnography. Moreover, this effort by AI would be indistinguishable from how anthropologists currently practice it.

The criticism against data science has long existed in anthropology. From Geertz's admonition against computation and a formalist analysis that would allow one to algorithmically "pass for a native" (2000, 11), to even more recent efforts of anthropologists attempting to mitigate, balance, or counterpose data learning with human learning, digital anthropologists acknowledge the gap. Nick Seaver (2018) discusses the problem as the "analog slot." He explains how anthropologists have "accommodated" computer science investigations by positioning ethnography conducted by humans as a "patched in alternative" or complement to computers in a series of contrasts: "the small-scale to [data's] large scale; the cultural to [data's] technical; thick description to [data's] thin description; the human to [data's] computer" (Seaver 2018, 380). In these parallels, ethnography conducted by a human is considered a complementary counterpoint to algorithmic systems, "a position nominally opposed to the digital, but which depends on it for coherence" (Seaver 2018, 380).

Yet, what Seaver and others bring to light is that while academic scholars assume that AI is cold, autonomous, rule-bound, inhuman, and aloof, there is always a person behind the algorithm, tweaking and adapting the algorithm, for better or worse. At Google, a "human" problem became evident when earlier versions of Google Photos automatically tagged a Black person and his Black friend as "gorillas" (Crawford 2016). The problem wasn't the algorithm and its error in making an accurate facial recognition. It was the programmers behind the algorithm who were complicit—as it was overwhelmingly white males who wrote the program with very little data compiled for African American faces, compared to the large trove of White people's faces. The real problem with AI, writes Crawford (2016) is that "Sexism, racism and other forms of discrimination are being built into the machine-learning algorithms that underlie the technology behind many 'intelligent' systems that shape how we are categorized and advertised to." In other examples, she points to errors made by Nikon's camera software, which misread images of Asian people as blinking, or in Hewlett-Packard's web camera software, which had difficulty recognizing people with dark skin tones.

This problem is exacerbated in law enforcement, where, as Crawford mentions, "Police departments across the United States deploy data-driven risk-assessment tools that are programmed by AI, in 'predictive policing' crime prevention efforts." In cities such as New York, Los Angeles, Chicago, and Miami, software analysis of large sets of historical crime data forecast where crime hot spots are most likely to emerge; the police are then directed to those areas. At the very least, this software risks perpetuating a vicious circle, in which the police increase their presence in the same places they are already policing (or over policing), thus ensuring that more arrests come from those same areas. In the United States, this could result in increased surveillance in traditionally poorer, non-white neighborhoods, while wealthy White neighborhoods are scrutinized less. Predictive AI programs are only as good as the data they are trained on, and that data has a complex history. Programmers make software that learns to program itself, and it learns from data that is inputted. As these algorithms learn from data, they can be considered "actants," connected to more-than-human networks. "Algorithms are then themselves agentic counterparts to their designers, not just their creations" (Seaver 2018, 378).

Anthropologists need to move into *creating* algorithms where they can aid in integrating data science and ethnography—not as parallel complements of thick data to thick description (Wang 2013), or as making up for the other, to fill in the gap, as the "analog slot", but as methods and forms of cultural analysis *integrated together*. Ironically, in the mid-1980s, anthropologists were criticized for "writing culture" in singular authored texts that assumed an authoritative voice for the informant. Now we need anthropologists to *write code* for algorithms, to bring back into data analysis humanistic perspectives with a concern for racial, gender, and social equality. Data science and ethnography have much in common with each other in their mutual approaches to human research. If anthropologists are not just "the humans" aside, conducting ethnography to complement or supplement data science, but, rather, are the agents *actively designing and training* these machine-learning systems, our society can perhaps reduce ingrained forms of bias built into artificial intelligence systems of the future.

The good news, as Stephen Paff (2021) details, both ethnography and data science have much in common in their mutual approaches to interpretation. Both ethnography and data science offer abductive approaches to cultural understanding; they both refine or reformulate ideas (conceptualization) in an iterative learning process; they both seek out patterns that emerge from the raw data. John Curran (2013, 70) likewise advocates for their similarities when he compares new forms of big data that apply machine-learning techniques with ethnography. Machine learning and ethnography, he claims, have a shared mutual interest and focus in producing cultural interpretations:

- both are interested in the everyday culture;
- both explore patterns, movement, and networks;
- both are interested in the physical—how the body interacts with products and space;
- both can attempt to understand taste in relation to consumption and life choices;
- both can offer holistic and synchronic approaches to analysis.

The point is, machine learning doing analysis is largely equivalent to practicing anthropologists doing ethnography, as both discover new material, come up with new concepts and ideas, and adapt their findings from patterns as they go along. In this way, machine learning, like ethnography, is "bottom up;" it is situational (contextually relevant), iterative (adaptive), and local. Ultimately, what makes data science like ethnography is that neither can be reduced to one or several methodologies, but, rather, they each combine a multitude of ways to learn that are always modified in a loose decentralized amalgam of various people, epistemologies, and methods—resulting in a "bastard" (Seaver 2015) approach to each situation.

USING AI AND ETHNOGRAPHY TO UNDERSTAND "NEW NORDIC" CUISINE IN DENMARK

To test out the similarities and synergies between ethnography and data science, Anders Munk and Anne-Kirstine Ellern conducted a qualitative–quantitative study of the New Nordic cuisine in Denmark. His approach was not to conduct two separate and distinct parallel studies, but one overlapping integrated investigation.

Noting the popularity of the "New Nordic Diet" in 2010, the famous Nordic restaurant, Noma, had dethroned El Bulli in Catalunya as the World's Best Restaurant on the annual top 50 list in a UK media publication, bringing a surge of chefs and fine-dining lovers to Copenhagen in search of the new Nordic revolution. To study how the New Nordic cuisine "revolution" developed as a cultural, political, and gastronomic phenomenon, Munk began by mapping the Scandinavian culinary web (Munk and Ellern, 2015; Munk, 2019). From a landscape of culinary communities of interest with different issue commitments Munk compared data driven insights with ethnographic accounts.

First, a part of his algorithm clustered mentions from websites in the inner parts of urban areas, where the New Nordic Movement is largely cited and celebrated, typically governmental and national in scope. Another part of his algorithm scanned data from food producers, local authorities, and other local food actors. A pattern of distinction emerged when mapping traces at scale and seemed to tell a positive story about the emergence of a new Nordic agenda run by political figures and other tangential food agendas. Yet, Munk postulated that he cannot discern the plot of the story or begin to understand its characters on one dimension of research alone.

He then conducted complementary ethnographic work in Danish rural regions, revealing a different pattern. What he discovered in ethnographic research was talk about local production by farmers rather than discussion of new Nordic cuisine. Speaking with dairy farmers, reindeer herders, or people selling smoked whale meat from the fjords outside the city, he found that none was familiar with the concept of New Nordic Food. Rather, they talked about their products as small scale and locally sourced.

Their findings reveal the New Nordic Food movement in Denmark has come to signify a politicized transition back to local food production. The research shows efforts of administrators, restaurants, and political figures at rebranding small-scale local producers and encouraging them to grow into export businesses that would help develop the economy—a highly politicized move that locals were not aware of, but government agencies were.

This large- and small-scale study tells a compelling story that each alone would not reveal. Machine learning adapted language as it learned phrases, "new Nordic", "locally produced", "organic", or "sustainable," to target smaller websites and locate specific expressions of this used to promote restaurants, food marts, and other sources in the investigation. Ethnographic work showed locals unaware of the movement but interested in promoting their locally sourced food. Deeper learning of social issues, politicized agendas and food movements is, thus, improved by deep ethnographic learning and broader machine learning with scope, involving multiple sites of inquiry, not possible with traditional ethnography or even multi-visits in current practicing anthropology.

By formulating algorithms and developing work with machine learning, anthropologists have their own unique approach to exploring social issues through data-intensive analysis. Anthropologists can inject their own epistemological (ways of learning and knowing) foundations for exploratory data practices that differ from machine learning and data techniques that are not humanistic in concept. Then practicing anthropology can be centered on providing interventions and solving problems that change the world, while, at the same time, engaging in public debates to bring a greater awareness and purpose of anthropology to society.

AI FOR ANTHROPOLOGICAL ENTREPRENEURS

The vast number of changes in the digital landscape also affords anthropologists exciting new opportunities to make a difference and solve real social problems as entrepreneurs in developing new business ventures and start-ups. New demand for emerging opportunities shifts the focus away from traditional models of anthropology as services-based research consultancies, to developing new digital products and services that are AI empowered as digital-first organizations.

The new generation of digital products, developed by data scientists and anthropologists working together, are AI based systems that assist in the machine interpretation of culture. For instance, automated digital ethnography (ADE) and AI-enabled multimodal analysis are tools that can assist businesses collect and analyze consumer and UX data and help develop a comprehensive understanding of their digital consumer base. Similarly, discipline-specific large language models (LLMs) and anthropological knowledge graphs can provide an interpretation of digital data gathered and help generate insights and recommendations based on the interpretation, such as making sense of social media discourse.

These tools help new business firms lead to innovative marketplace solutions. They afford researchers real-time insights into online consumer behavior, the shifting dynamics of digital communities, and the emergence of digital cultures, thereby facilitating more insightful and protectable strategic positions. These AI developed products help anthropologists start up new business consultancies that solve real social issues and make a difference as business entrepreneurs in the digital space, as demonstrated by the digital start-up, Artmatcher.

MAKING ART ACCESSIBLE TO ALL

Matt Artz, a digital anthropologist and entrepreneur, co-founded a digital company, Artmatcher, that uses AI assisted products to confront the challenge of inequalities in the art marketplace. Currently, the competitive art market in the digital space does not offer new and innovative artists access and equity to the market, but favors a winner-take-all approach, where popular artists continue to receive the majority of recommendations. Online art markets currently rely on machine learning recommender systems that are designed to suggest to viewers art pieces based on user preferences, resulting in the "rich-get-richer" dynamics. This algorithm bias leads to an unfair "loop" where popular artists and their artworks get recommended more often, while lesser-known artists remain obscure. This bias of inequality in the art scene limits chances for discovery and innovation for new artists, creating an unfairly biased environment against those without access.

Artz designed Artmatcher as an AI assisted digital product that helps level the playing field for all art enthusiasts. He developed and patented[4] a machine-learning algorithm for Artmatcher that works as a gamified participatory recommender system. This algorithm redefines the approach to art recommendations by augmenting traditional machine learning models with concepts of participation, actively rewarding behaviors of artists' promotion, rather than building off exclusionary factors of reputation. By valuing users' active involvement and participation, the system helps cultivate a sense of equity and inclusiveness in the platform. The experience for artists is also gamified, which means that the more users engage with Artmatcher, the more visibility and influence they earn within the art community.

His approach ensures that interactions enrich not only the experience of the individual user but also the entire Artmatcher community. Importantly, new artists are able to get recognition and foster a sense of community and participation in a platform where everyone has an equitable chance to engage, learn, and succeed, regardless of background. Ultimately, it's about making Artmatcher a place where creativity thrives, and everyone's art is seen.

AI and emerging new digital technologies are, thus, fundamental to the research and design of equitable start-ups like Artmatcher. As with all digital technologies, continuous improvement is necessary to keep a competitive edge. Recently, the company collaborated with art fairs to create a unique "phygital" experience (physical + digital). To iteratively improve that experience, they harnessed data scraping to capture social media reactions and then paired that data with app reviews, app analytics, and follow-up qualitative approaches to pinpoint areas of improvement and opportunities for testing with follow-up events. These active improvements help redefine the experience and accessibility of art for all.

AUTONOMOUS DRIVING CARS AND AI

While self-driving cars appear to be a new frontier in technological automation and artificial intelligence, the concept has been around for quite a while. Autonomous vehicles (AV) represent what Sarah Pink (2021, 307–324) describes as a "digital futures technology" that is "not quite complete," "always in-the-making," and "almost" about to break forth and change our world. Indeed, autonomous cars were the most hyped new emerging technology in 2015, and still are being reported frequently in business and technology media.

The idea of self-driving cars is appealing, since the popular media narrative of innovation taps into an imagined future, where our everyday lives are transformed by automation, emphasizing safety, increased personal time, and environmental benefits. The narrative of the automated car imagines us harmoniously synchronizing our lives, part of the "internet of things" and giving us more free time. Yet, driving is precisely the sort of everyday social activity through which people shape the culture of their community, and why it poses such a problem for automated cars. Driving is extremely social and comprises different social dynamics, depending on cultural meanings and different geographical regions, which make it a prime topic for anthropologists to investigate.

Driving appears to be governed by universal (inter)national traffic laws and traffic signals we all learn and know to obey. Turn signs notify us of changes in the road ahead, stop signs signal the driver to halt and look both ways before proceeding. But driving is also shaped by social and communal norms. If enough people adopt the same driving style, then that behavior hardens into a communal disposition. As David Brooks (2018) comments, once people understand what is normal in an area, more people tend to drive that way, and patterns become amplified: kindness breeds kindness; aggression breeds aggression. While driving cultures present an issue for self-driving cars since driving styles vary greatly in the US, even from city to city, they present a greater challenge for AI.

Melissa Cefkin, an anthropologist and formerly Principal Scientist and Senior Manager at Nissan Research in Silicon Valley, CA, discussed at a Las Vegas Auto Show in 2017[5] the challenges of creating AI equipped autonomous cars that operate smoothly in a human landscape. "What we're trying to generate are robotic cars essentially that work in teamwork with people." The challenge, she states, is blending and adapting the vehicle to work with humans, to take advantage of technology, but not take away complete control from the driver. "It's a core question of building teamwork between the robot and the people."

With new advances in AI, the focus of AVs has shifted from a utilitarian perspective of improving the functionality of self-driving cars to exploring new forms of human–robotic social interaction. It's no longer how can AV cars simply replicate or replace the work of human drivers, but how can AI and people work together in co-evolution of hybrid augmentations? AI must engage and negotiate with other humans such as pedestrians, bicyclists, motorcyclists, fellow drivers, and even passengers in the vehicle, in dynamic unpredictable contexts. In other words, self-driving cars must function not just like a car in public spaces; they must cooperate like humans.

What happens at a busy urban intersection with multiple cars arriving at or near the same time, and pedestrians attempting to cross the intersection slowly or another person abruptly runs across the street? Cefkin states (2017), in a future with fully driverless vehicles if there's no driver (in the vehicle) and you're trusting (AI) to interpret that social situation and make the same judgments that you would, but you can't make eye contact with people and there's nobody there to look at, as a pedestrian or another driver, what's going to happen? We need to understand how interactions will happen between autonomous vehicles and all other road users, from the outside as well as what it means for the people in the car.

Under various normal driving conditions, there is much eye contact and non-verbal exchange we take for granted. Cefkin continues,

People try to confirm that they've been seen. There is a lot of eye gazing and acknowledgement. We can tell people are kind of 'social listening': their pace might change among pedestrians, and as for vehicles with drivers, they are trying to make sure they've been seen so that people often communicate both directly and indirectly in order to clarify the order of things and their actions. People dynamically adjust their actions based on what's happening on the road.

(Cefkin, 2017)

Cefkin works with data scientists at Nissan to figure out how human perception translates into AI machine learning for the car. She helps create algorithmic programs that make AI cars more human-like. The challenge is first understanding how human intelligence works. We use our perception to identify, perceive and then experience phenomena in the world. We name objects and categorize them, giving them specific identities that help organize the world, as we decide what kind of thing this is: "Is it safe or dangerous? Is it cute and cuddly, or is it something that makes me angry?"

We begin to organize those kinds of experiences based on what we perceive so we can make decisions about what actions to take. But once a decision is made, then we must act on it and control it. This happens in split seconds. Since cognition is a highly complex act that is non-linear and situationally specific, designers of AI need to build in a level of predictability and outward readability, so that other people on the road or in the car know what to expect, which is necessary to build a level of public trust.

Nissan is experimenting and testing concept cars with different types of external signaling methods on the car to build trust. For instance, a text display in the car or a blue strip could be used for people outside to view, thus considering how something like external lighting might be broadcast to everybody. These signals would replace drivers' facial expressions and direct eye contact to signal the same message to everybody and be visible from all sides. In the future, a complete color-coded signaling system on AV cars might signal to people what state the car is in, especially for an autonomous mode of self-driving car.

The development of public trust in AVs will also change the urban landscape in cities. So far, robotic applications of AVs have operated in controlled or semi-controlled urban environments with relatively limited human interaction. Across the US, city and state governments have varied responses to allowing AVs testing opportunities. In 2015, when Arizona allowed for the testing of autonomous cars on selected public roads, the state governor received significant public backlash following the death of a woman cyclist after a collision with a driverless Uber test vehicle in Tempe (Bissell 2018). Public resistance to road testing of AVs has increased, and companies such as Waymo have endured threats against workers because of social unease (Greene 2018).

Cefkin states that under normal driving conditions, an AV should be able to navigate intersections, crosswalks, and all sorts of different settings. Nonetheless, there are occasions when an AV will encounter obstacles or challenging situations that would cause it to have a significant pause and to need additional support. AVs still depend on seamless autonomous mobility (SAM) systems and external human operators that can quickly assess a situation and address what's happening. Humans can send a recommendation to the car about what it should do, to move seamlessly through the encounter. Thus, we are reminded that AI driverless cars are not fully autonomous but require at times a larger network of humans to intervene.

Beyond the immediacy of a particular road situation, AV systems must involve the direct and indirect intervention of politics in local and state governments, which have their own rules and regulations and driverless car company politics. The politics of testing AVs operate according to social norms and regulations in different communities. For example, three different cities, San Francisco, CA, Tokyo, Japan, and Dubai in the United Arab Emirates are each interested in experimenting with urban "robotic applications" such as self-driving cars.

At issue in these three cities is how automatic systems such as AVs can integrate with urban environments and the extent to which they can become embedded in everyday life. San Francisco is interested in AVs with a start-up approach for use in small scale service delivery platforms; Tokyo would apply a large-scale national rollout across Japan developed with aid from large supplier firms; Dubai is interested in AVs for applications in modernizing public transport for a more segmented urban living (see While et al. 2021). Cefkin comments "we look globally (at Nissan) to understand how vehicle systems have different road systems, so that everyday practices on the road vary from place to place." Cars encounter situations that require negotiation with everybody else on that road, challenging car makers to build out responsible reactions to what Cefkin calls a "socially acceptable approach to autonomous systems." In the future, "smart cities" fitted with urban systems of automation will need to accommodate the interrelations among multiple active agents, reminding us that autonomous cars do not act alone, but are moving "mechanic assemblages" that comprise complex systems with multiple components that are economic, political, material, and semiotic, and are always evolving (Guattari 1996, 126).

Research conducted by anthropologists, data scientists and other social scientists thus shows that fully automated cars are still a work in progress. At issue are concerns over public trust in AVs, different car cultures, social driving patterns that vary by community and cityscape, national politics and corporate economic agendas, and questions of making AI more human-like in perception and actions. While new intelligent technologies such as AVs promise an imagined utopia in near future narratives of harmonious coexistence, AVs in a practical sense represent a technology that is "incomplete and unfinished" (Pink 2021, 317) and is not yet fully available to the public.

DRONES: ETHNOGRAPHIES OF THE AIR

In another not-yet-complete technology, human remote controlled and AI empowered drones offer anthropologists an intriguing cultural artifact that promises to alter everyday life and instigate social change in undetermined ways. In popular media, drones draw attention as indeterminate ambiguous entities, where definitions are uncertain but attitudes towards them are specific: "… we don't just think about drones. We all have feelings about drones" (Atherton et al. 2014). Indeed, drones may be one of the most equivocal, liminal, and polarizing emerging technologies that can be used for noble or nefarious purposes.

On a positive side, drones can deliver crucial medicines, needed supplies, food and water to hard-to-reach populations, whether for the reconnaissance of injured soldiers, stranded hikers in mountainous settings, or communities living in rural or remote locations. In healthcare and assisted living situations, drones can help deliver goods to those in need with less access to transportation and can operate under severe weather conditions. Drones for business can assist with mapping and designing large-scale warehouses and factories. They can track inventory by using AI that performs a depth analysis on current stock via flight videos. Drones with AI analytics scan shelves and automatically track and order new inventory. Drone flights can even be programmed to perform tasks during off-hours and dock themselves when work is complete. Amazon has experimented extensively with drone service, delivering textbooks, medical supplies, and even pizza. Matternet, a developer of a global drone delivery system, announced it has begun test operations on a five-kilometer route over the city of Zurich, Switzerland. This route is the world's longest drone delivery route over a major city and is used to transport diagnostic samples between two hospitals. The new test route showcases the potential for more efficient and streamlined patient care through the on-demand delivery of diagnostic samples and will serve as a template for expansion networks in Europe, the US, and beyond (Press release 2022[6]).

But the negative side of drones is their increased use in surveillance of illegal activities, policing of urban areas, and their popular application in warfare for delivering deadly payloads to designated targets. The US government routinely flies drones to patrol along the US–Mexican border, detecting migrant populations who illegally enter US territories. Drones are already set to become the central surveillance technology for policing peripheral spaces and "paranoid borders" of "less desirable surplus populations" (Shaw 2016). Ian Shaw further imagines a dystopian future where advances in AI enable small-scale nano-drones to fly in clustered formations of constellations, called "swarms", conducting predictive policing in urban settings. "With an ability to swarm in roving robotic clouds, the nano-drone holds the potential to pervade, saturate, and modulate the urban volume in a way that neither the helicopter nor CCTV can adequately perform" (2016, 25). These potentially armed small drones of predictive policing could move inside workplaces, perch inside of homes, undetected, presenting a frightening AI future for urban habitants. This conundrum over a new technology—bane or boon—makes the study of drones highly anticipatory for anthropologists.

DRONES IN ANTHROPOLOGICAL RESEARCH

Anthropologists have defined a new frontier for cultural investigation using drones, termed atmospheric anthropology or "ethnographies of the air" (Fish et al. 2017, 248). This includes the atmosphere as a medium for epistemological projects and methodological experimentation. Drones provide access to cultural activities with a kind of actual "bird's eye view" in urban research (While et al. 2021) which has, until now, been only a metaphor for passive ethnographic observation of a particular field site. The view-from-above perspective of drone life provides anthropologists with insights into characteristics of landscapes unseen by the terrestrial eye. Like airplanes, satellites, and other types of atmospheric archaeology, drones offer specific types of remote sensing from the air. Drones flown from lower elevation with high-definition cameras and other remote sensing payloads offer high-resolution images. Easier to deploy and less expensive than satellites or airplanes, drones offer a democratization of atmospheric remote sensing.

In arial research, besides mapping out settlements, archaeologists use drones to measure 3D generated topographical models (Meyer et al. 2016), photograph rock art (Mark and Billo 2016), and rapidly collect data on threatened sites (Willis et al. 2016). Oakland University professor Jon Carroll is part of a pioneering team of anthropology practitioners harnessing the latest advances in drone technology to promote sustainable agriculture. His use of drones helps fight the spread of disease and combats hunger in parts of Africa. Professor Carroll recently traveled to Liwonde, Malawi to work on a research project helping farmers boost crop production in the face of climate change. The project, called "Precision Agriculture for Smallholder Systems in Africa," is part of Feed the Future, the US government's global hunger and food security initiative.[7]

Drones fitted with high tech equipment can survey the land through high-precision aerial photography and help researchers assess crop health. The communities in Malawi that surround the irrigation scheme are heavily dependent on water-intensive crops, such as rice, which causes puddles to form in the fields. Carroll and his research team use drones to work closely with residents to collect the aerial and ground data from drones. Through digitally enhanced multispectral aerial images of the farm field, digital technology aids Carroll and other researchers to "see" green areas significantly better for discerning plant health. The drone imagery helps irrigation engineers and agriculturalists develop topical strategies from the aerial perspective that allow water to better flow through the irrigation scheme more efficiently, avoiding stagnation, which enables mosquitoes to breed and cause disease. This technology can continually build on his research and improve the lives of potentially millions of people.

The application of drones goes beyond agriculture to include politically motivated forms of mapping and counter-mapping—or the production of alternative cultural boundaries. NGOs (nongovernmental organizations) are beginning to buy their own drones. For example, the World Wildlife Federation has announced that it will use drones to track rhinoceros poachers in more remote locations in Africa. But this raises the ethical question that in the future drones could be armed with guns or lasers to kill or disable poachers who are out of the reach of thinly stretched law enforcement on the ground.

DRONES IN WARFARE: HUNTING WITHOUT FIGHTING

Drone use is increasingly popular in modern warfare, which anthropologists also study. The US has deployed drones over Iran, Iraq, Afghanistan, Yemen, Pakistan, Libya, Somalia, and Syria, and routinely flies them to patrol the US–Mexican border. The criticism of drone warfare is that the drone operators sit next to intelligence officers and watch a live video feed from the drone's camera. Some say this is highly unethical when the operator is miles away from the scene of combat action. The way the Predator and Reaper drones, two popular models used in combat, operate is more like hunting than warfare, since there is no chance that the drone's operator can be attacked by his adversary. Anthropologists studying this admonish that such encounters project an intimate quality that is one-sided and asymmetrical: the target does not even know he is being observed, when the drone operator can see him close up, reclining on the roof of his house. "Without even knowing he is in combat, he is killed as if by a thunderbolt from the sky." Anthropologist Hugh Gusterson claims, "Weapon and warrior were more or less coincident in space. Drones have disarticulated the spatial relationship between weapon and warrior" (2014, 196). This "dissociative" style of killing makes the taking of life too easy, removed from surroundings of war. Still, drone operators seem to suffer high rates of PTSD.

But others say the use of drones in warfare saves lives. If an unmanned plane is shot down or crashes for other reasons, the pilot's life will not be lost, since the pilot will be thousands of miles away from the plane. Moreover, military pilots are expensive to train, and, as the American public is increasingly resistant to deaths of servicemen, reducing casualty rates becomes much more popular. Another factor is cost—each predator drone costs roughly $5 million dollars, a much cheaper option than a $150 million fighter jet such as the F-16. A third issue, writes Gusterson (2014), is tactical. Drones can hover for about 40 minutes in the same location and zoom in on their camera to identify targets much more easily than a quick fly-by fighter jet. This ability to dwell in an area for a while makes it more accurate for analyzing patterns on the ground to collect a damage assessment before deciding on whether to strike.

NEW AI CAPABILITIES OF DRONES

AI has greatly expanded the capabilities of drones. Until recently, drones were only able to display what their cameras captured. Now, with AI software, drones can perceive their surroundings, map areas, track objects and provide analytical feedback in real time. Drones are social tools for mapping and measuring topography, but also cultural objects with powerful potential for businesses, scientists, activists, and military uses, making them highly problematic cultural topics of interest for anthropologists.

For instance, new technology uses deep learning networks that help military drones sift through multiple faces in crowds to find and identify persons of interest, or specific targets. Deep learning uses multilayered structures of algorithms or neural networks to scan crowds for an individual. Algorithms in drones would then attempt to draw similar conclusions as soldiers would remotely, by continually analyzing data with facial recognition programming for a given military scenario. The troubling possibility for the future of smart AI drones will be when such technology is given full autonomy to select and target humans on their own. As we look to the future, we can expect drone technology to proliferate as countries such as Russia, China, India, and Saudi Arabia start using drones against people, such as what is occurring in the Russia–Ukraine war.

There remain many regulatory issues and technological limitations against the full roll-out of drones, other than current applications for archaeological, agriculture, or military use. Drones represent a "digital futures" subject of an emerging but still incomplete technology (Pink 2022), which is led by future utopian visions, but remains uncertain. Like self-driving cars, this technology is aided by popular narratives of innovation and imagination that exist in a world of the future where unlimited services and conveniences are just around the corner to make life easier. But, in reality, both AVs and drones are technologies that are incomplete in a practical sense. Concerns over privacy, ethics of use in wartime and surveillance, legality of air space and functional issues of battery life and extendibility make drones the subject of "ongoingness," unfinished and incomplete. Drones continue to hold a fascination in public discourse as uncertain objects that bring both admiration and fear.

CONCLUSION

The growth of digital anthropology and new technology promises practicing anthropologists and students exciting challenges and opportunities that will impact society and shape anthropological pedagogy in years to come. Digital anthropology is poised to play a significant role in the ways our futures become entangled with these emerging technologies. Bridging an ethnographic sensibility of anthropology with the latest AI research techniques, anthropologists can intervene and help shape new technologies to make a positive difference in the world. Students and practitioners will need to incorporate the latest theories and methods of digital anthropology with traditional anthropological theories into business practices, design fields and organizational culture, and new start-up ventures. By integrating digital anthropology into the discourse and practice of business anthropology, anthropologists will enhance their ability to collect and interpret data on a scale previously unimaginable, offering society the means to generate richer insights and more informed recommendations. In this way, anthropologists can employ data science in thoughtful, humanistic ways to encourage public conversations and make anthropology relevant, addressing pressing social issues with the explicit goal of fostering real social change.

NOTES

1 Some useful definitions: artificial intelligence (AI) is a general term that refers to techniques that enable computers to mimic human behavior. It is a program or network of programs using algorithms designed to sense, reason, act, and adapt. An algorithm is a procedure or method by which the AI system conducts its task, usually to create a "model" in which to analyze data. Machine learning represents a set of algorithms trained on data that make all of this possible. In machine learning, the performance of the algorithms improves as they are exposed to more data over time. Deep learning is a type of machine learning, inspired by the structure of the human brain in which multilayered neural networks learn from vast amounts of data (also called neural networks). Deep learning is a subset of machine learning, which is a subset of AI.

2 Some are now referring to it as digital materialities (see Pink et al. 2016).

3 A number of significant books, including Clifford and Marcus (1986), Marcus and Fisher (1986), Clifford (1988), and Said (1973, 1978) addressed this predicament of cultural analysis.

4 https://patents.google.com/patent/US20230046646A1/en?inventor=Matthew+R.+Artz.

5 See YouTube discussion, https://www.youtube.com/watch?v=6koKuDegHAM

6 https://www.businesswire.com/news/home/20221212005097/en/Matternet
-Launches-World%E2%80%99s-Longest-Urban-Drone-Delivery-Route-Co
nnecting-Hospitals-and-Laboratories-in-Zurich-Switzerland

7 https://oakland.edu/socan/news/2018/anthropology-professor-deploys-drone
-to-combat-hunger-in-africa.

CONCLUSION

This book has discussed anthropological ways of thinking in the form of cultural analysis applied to solving business problems in a range of settings. It hopes to provide value to those working in or for industry, government, the nonprofit sector or consulting work, in areas of consumer research, design concepts and UX, and organizational work culture practices. The field of business anthropology also purposefully addresses real social issues and, at times, seeks to encourage broad, public conversations about topics with the explicit goal of fostering social change. As detailed throughout this book, this makes business anthropology quite different from traditional, academically oriented anthropology in several ways:

First, traditional academic anthropology retains a scholarly distance from applied action, disengaged from practice as a critical observer. Academic anthropologists are involved in offering valuable critiques and thoughtful discussions of issues, but they typically do not offer recommendations, solutions, or even interventions to issues. In contrast, business anthropologists, like other anthropologists of practice, are involved in progressive action, seeking to implement solutions for change. They often coordinate their efforts with scholars in other fields, as well as with designers, corporate researchers, brand marketers, policy makers, and so forth, making collective efforts part of a larger multifaceted compendium of change. This also assumes a commitment and responsibility to carry out work on projects that are ethically sound and purposely involve other viewpoints to help eliminate solitary bias that can occur with traditional singular approaches.

DOI: 10.4324/9781003358930-7

Second, a conventional academically inclined perspective in anthropology focuses on existing social phenomena with a focus on the past. Academics typically explore what has occurred and led to a particular situation in which a people and society now exist. In contrast, the focus of anthropology fields, such as digital or design anthropology, begin with exploring applications of current technologies and designs and their impact on social situations that are continually moving on, and may also explore possibilities into yet unknown future circumstances. The narrative of technology is full of promise but, in reality, it is often incomplete, always evolving. For example, smartphones advance every year with new technological features, but are still subject to change, modification, and updates. The iPhone 14 boasts a new crash detection mode to protect users by signaling to emergency workers an imminent vehicle crash. However, iPhone users have complained of inadvertent crash activations, such as when taking a roller coaster ride in an amusement park or skiing downhill, and find that emergency workers are waiting for them at the end.[1] Reframing the "pinnacle of technology" as a continuously evolving project, challenges our ideas that technology is purchased and consumed as a finished social reality. It shows instead that much of new technology is never fully complete. Where issues configure and how they will impact society cannot be wholly predicted, but anthropologists of practice aim towards considering insights and ethical issues as they unfold in the making and adapting to new configurations as they become manifest.

Third, academic approaches in anthropology tend to view capitalism and all its associations in industries that operate for-profit, and even not-for-profit, as subversive, going against the grain of unbiased understanding and positive change. Much of this perspective still exists in higher levels of academia, even though anthropology and business are inextricably historically entangled in academia as well as in commerce. As Rita Denny and Patricia Sunderland remind us, a singular hegemonic view of capitalism is not useful, since "… business is not a monolith, neither inherently good or bad. Business, like anthropology, is made up of actors with strategic goals and interests, enmeshed in the material and practical realities, built up in the past and present" (Denny and Sunderland 2014, 18). But capitalism in academia is viewed negatively from the perspective of relations of inequality and power, such as between owners of capital and employees, or firms and markets, which are assumed to operate antagonistically to each other. As Laura Nader (1969), alerted us, traditional academic anthropologists typically "study down," investigating marginalized or underrepresented peoples, rather than "study up" at corporations, centers of power and influence, and the actors involved. Nevertheless, business anthropologists are hired by corporations to work within institutions of profit to improve employee relations and work practices. Anthropologists working in or for business note that exploitation of workers is not a structural given. Instead, with a focus on improving work conditions and fostering ideas of shared culture from within a firm, employees' lives are encouraged to become part of a collective whole, rather than assume they are exploited and alienated. This change in perspective opens the notion to dialogue, unrealized possibilities, and belonging to corporate communities, which challenges the idea of taken-for-granted structural domination, and subversive relations as unilaterally unequal and pervasive.

Fourth, traditional anthropological approaches to users and consumers in society view long-term fieldwork as necessary, fostering a sense of community with others and perhaps a traditional way for anthropologists to achieve a level of community acceptance with the people they study. However, business anthropologists and designers (Pink et al. 2016) advocate that this is not always necessary or even possible; and that it is not a defining feature of what makes for good anthropology. Studies in business anthropology are most often based on multiple short fieldwork events extended over multiple locations and even over time, that bring together partners and insights from different projects, people, and locations. Moreover, as Sarah Pink and colleagues (Pink et al. 2017) affirm, talking to experts in the field shortens the time it takes to "discover" insights on your own. Experts are sources of idea generation as well as potential collaborators in projects, so their long-term commitment to a subject matter becomes an asset, in place of the lone anthropologist spending lengthy time to learn something new.

Fifth, most practicing anthropologists also challenge the status quo of traditional anthropology by actively inviting collaboration. Rather than the lone anthropologist out in the field collecting data individually on "her" or "his" people, as is traditionally done, business anthropologists engage with other disciplines and other people, such as web designers, engineers, designers, advertising creatives, policy makers, and AI programming itself, that are part of the contemporary world and commercial industry. This collaborative approach to practice forces a change from a self-referential and insular perspective common to traditional anthropology, to one that is more "outwardly" focused and engaged with others. As business anthropologists work with others on projects and move from one project to another, they also transition in and out of creative spaces, "intermittently working with clients, research participants, and other colleagues who have different concepts, languages, and worldviews. In this fluid space, they listen to multiple voices, gain insider views, and communicate across boundaries" (McCabe 2013, 160). Business anthropologists gain a rich, multi-voiced perspective on a variety of issues, where meanings are often negotiated, refreshed, and collaborative. This shifts the focus away from the singular, authoritative voice of the lone anthropologist, to a more collaborative and negotiated plurality of voices in the social production of knowledge. And when anthropologists do partner with governments, industry, and social activism to promote positive change, their intervention isn't limited to the singular project at hand, but may, at times, go "beyond the project" (Pink et al. 2022, 3), extending beyond the specific needs of a client and stakeholders, to influence additional projects or build towards other possible futures and how they might be imagined, narrated, and enacted.

I conclude with remarks from Brian Moeran's thoughtful "Coda," (2012, 290–297) in what unifies or should unify and define the field of business anthropology when we discuss culture, the economy, and social change. First, Moeran states business anthropology must engage with theory—which is done through "examination, questioning, analysis, comparison, rephrasing" (2012, 293) the work of other scholars, practitioners, designers, and so forth who challenge the status quo—and our own ideas on a subject; this engagement, secondly, should invite comparison of how their work compares to ours and others. A holistic approach, comparing our work in one location or type of business with another will continuously challenge and help redefine terms such as "business," "capitalism," "work culture," "design concepts," and so forth. Third, Moeran states that we must also continuously evolve our methodologies. This means we seek to integrate and continuously adapt and integrate new methods in our work, such as joining AI and machine learning with classic ethnographic approaches. Since business anthropologists are at the forefront of trends, we are the ones to challenge conventions in capitalism, business practices, social justice, our own ideas, and others. And, finally, we must bring in anthropological theory—in a classic sense of revitalizing terms such as animism, totemism, social dramas, magic, the gift, and so forth—which continues anthropology's undertaking in the classic sense of making the strange familiar, and familiar strange. This would also allow us "to render visible to the public what so often remains invisible about business" and other social processes (2012, 295).

Businesses are constantly in search of more information, more data, much of it broad but thin. Anthropology provides thick data that deepens business understanding. Providing deep understanding is also how anthropology, in a more public voice, can call attention to subtle or taken-for-granted issues on social injustice, gender inequalities, environmental concerns, and more equitable goals for society and the world. Tied to industry, business anthropologists can offer thoughtful leadership and actionable change in the world at a time when it is most needed. In these ways, business anthropologists can be at the forefront of change, to hopefully overcome our own divisions and unite as anthropologists and become a clear and powerful public expression of why anthropology matters.

NOTE

1 https://www.wsj.com/articles/the-owner-of-this-iphone-was-in-a-sever e-car-crashor-just-on-a-roller-coaster-11665314944

REFERENCES

Anderson, Benedict 2016. *Imagined Communities: Reflections on the Origin and Spread of Nationalism*. New York: Verso.

Appadurai, Arjun 1986. *The Social Life of Things*. Cambridge: Cambridge University Press.

Appadurai, Arjun 1996. *Modernity At Large: Cultural Dimensions of Globalization*. Ann Arbor, MI: University of Minnesota Press.

Artz, Matt 2022. Design Anthropology, Algorithmic Bias, Behavioral Capital, and the Creator Economy. *Practicing Anthropology*, 44(2): 33–36.

Artz, Matt 2023. From Machine Learning to Machine Knowing: A Digital Anthropology Approach for the Machine Interpretation of Cultures. UNESCO. Available at: https://unesdoc.unesco.org/ark:/48223/pf0000384902.

Atherton, Kelsey, Erin Biba, Brooke Borel, Rebecca Boyle, Clay Dillow, Emily Geertz, David Hambling, Jeremy Hsu, Gregory Mone, and Erik Sofge 2014. 25 Reasons to Love Drones, and 5 Reasons to Fear them, *Popular Science* (technology). Available at: https://www.popsci.com/article/technology/25-reasons-love-drones/.

Baba, Marietta 2012. Anthropology and Business: Influence and Interests. *Journal of Business Analytics*, 1(1): 20–71.

Baba, Marietta 2014. De-anthropologizing Ethnography: A Historical Perspective on the Commodification of Ethnography as a Business Service, in Rita Denny and Patricia Sunderland (eds), *Handbook of Anthropology in Business*. New York: Routledge, 43–68.

Bateson, Gregory, D. D. Jackson, J. Haley, and J. H. Weakland 1963. A Note on the Double Bind—1962. *Family Process*, 2: 154–161.

Belk , Russell 2020. *Little Luxuries: Decency, Deservingness and Delight*, in Timothy Malefyt and Maryann McCabe (eds), *Women, Consumption and Paradox*. London: Routledge, 239–252.

Belk, Russell, Eileen Fischer, and Robert Kozinets 2013. *Qualitative Consumer and Marketing Research*. London: Sage.

Benedict, Ruth 1947. *Race, Science and Politics*. New York: Viking Press.

Berg, Martin and Vaike Fors 2017. Workshop as Nodes of Knowledge Co-production: Beyond Ideas of Automagical Synergies, in Sarah Pink, Vaike Fors and Tom O'Dell (eds), *Theoretical Scholarship and Applied Practice*. New York: Berghahn Books, 53–72.

Bissell , David 2018. Automation Interrupted: How Autonomous Vehicle Accidents Transform the Material Politics of Automation. *Political Geography*, 65: 57–66.

Blomberg, Jeanette and Chuck Darrah 2015. A Seat at the Table of Social Change through Service Design. *Ethnographic Praxis in Industry Conference Proceedings*, 2015(1): 290–305, https://doi.org/10.1111/1559-8918.2015.01056.

Boellstorff , Tom 2015 (2008). *Coming of Age in Second Life: An Anthropologist Explores the Virtually Human*. Princeton, NJ: Princeton University Press.

Borofsky, Robert 2004. *Conceptualizing Public Anthropology*. Electronic document, https://web.archive.org/web/20070414153742/http://www.publica nthropology.org/Defining/definingpa.htm, April 11, 2007.

Borofsky, Robert 2018. Public Anthropology, in *The International Encyclopedia of Anthropology*. John Wiley. https://doi.org/10.1002/9781118924396. wbiea1899.

Bowker , Geoffrey and Susan Leigh Star 2000. *Sorting Things Out*. Cambridge, MA: MIT Press, DOI: https://doi.org/10.7551/mitpress/6352.001.0001.

boyd, danah and Kate Crawford 2012. Critical Questions for Big Data. *Information, Communication & Society*, 15(5): 662–679, doi:10.1080/1369118X.2012.678878.

Briody, Elizabeth K. 2013. Managing Conflict in Organizational Partnerships, in D. Douglas Caulkins and Ann T. Jordan (eds), *A Companion to Organizational Anthropology*. Malden, MA: Blackwell: 236–256.

Briody, Elizabeth K. 2014. Transforming Hospital Culture by Changing Discourse. *Journal of Business Analytics*, 3(2): 216–237.

Briody, Elizabeth K. and Robert T. Trotter II (eds) 2008. *Partnering for Organizational Performance: Collaboration and Culture in the Global Workplace*. Lanham, MD: Rowman & Littlefield.

Briody, Elizabeth K., Adam Gamwell, Phil Surles, JoAiken, and Dawn Lehman 2023. Ten Things about the Public Stage. Available at: https://www.anthropology-news.org/articles/ten-things-about-the-public-stage/, February 8, 2023.

Briody , Elizabeth and T. M. Pester 2017. Redesigning Anthropology's Ethical Principles to Align with Anthropological Practice, in Timothy Malefyt and Robert J. Morais (eds) *Ethics in the Anthropology of Business*, 23–43.

Briody, Elizabeth, Robert Trotter and Tracy Meerwarth 2010. *Transforming Culture: Creating and Sustaining a Better Manufacturing Organization*. New York: Palgrave Macmillan.

Brooks , David 2018. "How Would Jesus Drive? *New York Times*, Opinion | op-ed Columnist, Jan. 4.

Bruner, Edward M. 1986. Ethnography as Narrative, in Victor W. Turner and Edward M. Bruner (eds), *The Anthropology of Experience*, Urbana, IL: University of Illinois Press, 139–155.

Cefkin, Melissa 2017. *Anthropologist Dr. Melissa Cefkin Talks About Artifical Intelligence Autonomous Driving #CES2017*. Available at: https://www.you tube.com/watch?v=6koKuDegHAM.

Chussil, Mark 2016. "Rally the Troops" and Other Business Metaphors You Can Do Without. *Harvard Business Review*, November 24.

Clifford, James 1986. Introduction: Partial Truths, in James Clifford and George Marcus (eds), *Writing Culture: The Poetics and Politics of Ethnography*. Berkeley, CA: University of California Press, 1–26.

Clifford, James 1988. *The Predicament of Culture: Twentieth-century Ethnography, Literature, and Art*, Volume 1. Cambridge, MA: Harvard University Press.

Clifford, James and George Marcus 1986. *Writing Culture: The Poetics and Politics of Ethnography*. Berkeley, CA: University of California Press.

Cole, Calen and Carolyn Wei 2020. Growing Communities How Social Platforms Can Help Community Groups Achieve the Right Scale at the Right Time. *EPIC Proceedings*, 2020: 87–97, ISSN 1559–8918. Available at: https://www.epicpeople.org/epic.

Crawford , Kate 2016. Artificial Intelligence's White Guy Problem. *New York Times*, Opinion, June 25.

Curran , John 2013. Big Data or 'Big Ethnographic Data'? Positioning Big Data within the Ethnographic Space. *EPIC Proceedings*, 2013: 62–73.

DaCol, Giovanni and David Graeber 2011. Foreword: The Return of Ethno-graphic Theory. *HAU: Journal of Ethnographic Theory*, 1(1): vi–xxxv.

Denny, Rita and Patricia Sunderland (eds) 2014. *Handbook of Anthropology in Business*. London: Routledge.

Douglas, Mary 2002. *Purity and Danger: An Analysis of Concepts of Pollution and Taboo*, London: Routledge Classics.

Drazin , Adam 2021. *Design Anthropology in Context*. London: Routledge.

Ewart, Ian 2013. Designing by Doing: Building Bridges in the Highlands of Borneo, in Wendy Gunn, Ton Otto, Rachel Charlotte Smith (eds), *Design Anthropology: Theory and Practice*. London: Bloomsbury, 85–99.

Ferguson, Brian 2013. Full Spectrum: The Military Invasion of Anthropology, in Neil L. Whitehead and Sverker Finnström (eds), *Virtual War and Magical Death: Technologies and Imaginaries for Terror and Killing*. Durham, NC: Duke University Press.

Ferraro, Gary P. and Elizabeth K. Briody 2023. *The Cultural Dimension of Global Business* (9th edn). London: Routledge.

Ferryman, Kadija 2017. Reframing Data as a Gift. Available at SSRN: https://ssrn.com/abstract=3000631 or http://dx.doi.org/10.2139/ssrn.3000631.

Fish, Adam, Bradley Garrett and Oliver Case 2017. Drones Caught in the Net. *Imaginations Journal of Cross-Cultural Image Studies/revue d études interculturelle de l image*, 8(2), doi: doi:10.17742/IMAGE.LD.8.2.8. https://doi.org/10.17742/image.LD.8.2.8.

Fiske, Shirley and Robert Wulff 2022. Foreword: The Emergence of WAPA and Birth of Praxis, in Terry Redding and Charles Cheney (eds), *Profiles of Anthropological Praxis*. New York: Berghahn Books: x–xv.

Geertz Clifford 2000 (1973). *The Interpretation of Cultures*. New York: Basic Books.

Geiger, R. S. and D. Ribes 2011. *Trace Ethnography: Following Coordination through Documentary Practices*, 44th Hawaii International Conference on System Sciences, Kauai, HI, USA, 2011, pp. 1–10, doi:10.1109/HICSS.2011.455.

Geismar, Haidy and Hannah Knox (eds) 2021. *Digital Anthropology* (2nd edn). London: Routledge.

Goffman, Ervine 1959. *The Presentation of Self in Everyday Life*. New York: Doubleday.

Greene, Tristan 2018. Anti-robot Vigilantes in Arizona Try to Scare Off Waymo's Self-driving Cars. *Artifical Intelligence*, 13 December.

Guattari, Felix 1996 *The Guattari Reader* (Gary Genosko, ed.). Oxford: Blackwell.

Gunn, Wendy, T. Otto and Rachel Charlotte Smith (eds) 2013. *Design Anthropology*. London: Bloomsbury.

Gusterson, Hugh 2014. Toward an Anthropology of Drones: Remaking Space, Time, and Valor in Combat, in Matthew Evangelista and Henry Shue (eds), *The American Way of Bombing*, Ithaca, NY: Cornell University Press, 191–206.

Hallam, Elizabeth and Tim Ingold 2007. *Creativity and Cultural Improvisation*. Routledge: London.

Halse, Joachim 2013. Ethnographies of the Possible, in Wendy Gunn, Ton Otto, Rachel Charlotte Smith (eds), *Design Anthropology: Theory and Practice*. Abingdon: Routledge, 180–198.

Hamada Connolly, Tomoko 2015. On the Meaning(s) of Culture. *Journal of Business Anthropology*, 4(1): 125–129.

Hannertz, Ulf 2021. Postscript: A Letter to Anthropologists, in Gillian Tett (ed.), *Anthro-vision: A New Way to See in Business and Life*. New York: Simon and Schuster.

Hasbrouck , Jay 2018. *Ethnographic Thinking*. London: Routledge.

Hazen, Rebecca, Genny Mangum and Tom Souhlas 2020. Scaling Experience Measurement: Capturing and Quantifying User Experiences across the Real Estate Journey. *EPIC Proceedings*, 2020. ISSN 1559–8918, https://www.epicpeople.org/epic.

Heller , Monica 2016. Ethics as Institutional Process, in Dena Plemmons and Alex W. Barker (eds), *Anthropological Ethics in Context: An Ongoing Dialogue*. Walnut Creek, CA: Left Coast Press: 231.

Hempton, Gordon and John Grossmann 2009. *One Square Inch of Silence*. New York: Simon and Schuster.

Henshall , Stuart 2019. Perspectives: New Forms of Literacy are Expanding Digital Expression, available at: https://www.epicpeople.org/new-forms-of-literacy-are-expanding-digital-expression/.

Hillier, Katie 2023. Digital Anthropology meets Data Science. *Anthropology News* 64(2): 3–7.

Hine , Christine 2000. *Virtual Ethnography*. Thousand Oaks, CA: Sage.

Hoffer, Eric 2010. *The True Believer*. New York: Harper Perennial Modern Classics.

Holstein , James and Jaber Gubrium 1995. *The Active Interview*. Thousand Oaks, CA: Sage.

Howes, David 1987. Olfaction and Transition: An Essay on the Ritual Use of Smell. *Canadian Review of Sociology and Anthropology*, 24(3): 398–416.

Iglesias Kuntz, Lucía 2018. The Secrets of Tiwanaku, revealed by a drone. *The UNESCO Courier*, 64–72.

Ingold , Tim 2008. Anthropology is Not Ethnography. *Proceedings of the British Academy*, 154, 69–92. © The British Academy 2008.

Ingold , Tim 2013. *Making*. London: Routledge.

Ingold , Tim 2018. *Anthropology: Why it Matters*. Cambridge: Polity.

Jordan , Ann 2019. Business Anthropology, in *Oxford Research Encyclopedias, Anthropology*. https://doi.org/10.1093/acrefore/9780190854584.013.4.

Koons , Adam 2022. Emergency Food Security Recovery: An Afghanistan Case, in Terry Redding and Charles Cheney (eds), *Profiles of Anthropological Praxis*. New York: Berghahn Books: 7–20.

Koycheva, Lora V. 2023. Ethnography for an Accessible Future: Scaling Embodiment as a Paradigm for Anthropology in the Digital World through Telepresence Robots. France: UNESCO. Available at: https://unesdoc.unesco.org/ark:/48223/pf0000384899.

Kozinets, Robert 2002. Can Consumers Escape the Market? Emancipatory Illuminations from Burning Man. *Journal of Consumer Research*, 29(1): 20–38.

Kozinets, Robert 2009. *Netnography: Doing Ethnographic Research Online*. Thousand Oaks, CA: Sage.

Ladner , Sam 2014. *Practical Ethnography*. Thousand Oaks, CA: Left Coast Press.

Ladner , Sam 2019. *Mixed Methods*. Self published.

Lanzeni, Déborah, Karen Waltorp, Sarah Pink, and Rachel Charlotte Smith 2023. *An Anthropology of Futures and Technologies*. London:Routledge.

Lakoff , George and Mark Johnson 2003. *Metaphors We Live By*. Chicago: University of Chicago Press.

Latour, Bruno and Steve Woolgar 1986. *Laboratory Life: The Construction of Scientific Facts*. Princeton, NJ: Princeton University Press.

Levin, Nadine 2019. 10 Things You Should Know about Moving from Academia to Industry. Available at: https://www.epicpeople.org/10-things-you-should-know-about-moving-from-academia-to-industry/.

Lindley, Joseph, Dhruv Sharma, and Robert Potts 2014. Anticipatory Ethnography: Design Fiction as an Input to Design Ethnography. *Ethnographic Praxis in Industry Conference Proceedings*, 237–253, doi: doi:10.1111/1559-8918.01030.

Lo, Jenny and Steve Morseman 2018. The Perfect uberPOOL: A Case Study on Trade-Offs. *Ethnographic Praxis in Industry Proceedings*, ISSN 1559–8918, available at: https://www.epicpeople.org/intelligences.

Madsbjerg, Christian and Mikkel Rasmussen 2014. *The Moment of Clarity*. Brighton, MA:Harvard Business Review Press.

Malefyt, Timothy D. 2003. *Models, Metaphors and Client Relations: The Negotiated Meanings of Advertising*, in *Advertising Cultures*, Timothy de Waal Malefyt and Brian Moeran (eds), Oxford: Berg, 139–163.

*Malefyt, Timothy D. 2009Understanding the Rise of Consumer Ethnography: Branding Technomethodologies in the New Economy, *American Anthropologist*, 111(2): 201–210.

*Malefyt, Timothy D. 2014An Anthropology of the Senses: Tracing the Future of Sensory Marketing in Brand Rituals, in Rita Denny and Patricia Sunderland (eds), *Handbook of Anthropology in Business*. London:Routledge, 704–721.

Malefyt, Timothy de Waal and Robert J. Morais 2010. Creativity, Brands and the Ritual Process: Confrontation and Resolution in Advertising Agencies. *Culture and Organization*, 16(4): 333–347.

Malefyt, Timothy de Waal and Robert J. Morais 2012. *Advertising and Anthropology: Ethnographic Practice and Cultural Perspectives*. London: Berg.

Malefyt Timothy de Waal and Robert J.Morais 2017. Introduction: Capitalism, Work, and Ethics, in Timothy Malefyt and Robert Morais (eds), *Ethics in the Anthropology of Business*. New York: Routledge, 1–22.

Malinowski, Bronislaw 1926. *Sex and Repression in Savage Society*. London: Routledge.

Malinowski, Bronislaw 1927. *The Father in Primitive Psychology*. London: Norton.

Marcus, George 1995. Ethnography in/of the World System: The Emergence of Multi-sited Ethnography. *Annual Review of Anthropology*, 24: 95–117.

Marcus, George 2010. Holism and the Expectations of Critique in post-1980s Anthropology: Notes and Queries in Three Acts and an Epilogue, in Ton Otto and Nils Bubandt (eds), *Experiments in Holism*. Oxford: Wiley-Blackwell, 28–46.

Marcus, George and Michael Fisher 1986. *Anthropology as Cultural Critique: An Experimental Moment in the Human Sciences*. Chicago, IL: University of Chicago Press.

Mark, Robert and Evelyn Billo 2016. Low Altitude Unmanned Aerial Photography to Assist in Rock Art Studies. *The SAA Archaeological Record*, 16(2): 14–16.

Mauss, Marcel 2000. *The Gift*. New York: Norton.

McCabe, Maryann 2013"360 on Method", Opinions: Ethnographic Methods in the Study of Business. *Journal of Business Analytics*, 2(2): 133–167.

McCabe, Maryann and Rita Denny 2019. Anthropology in Consumer Research. Anthropology website, available at: https://doi.org/10.1093/acrefore/9780190854584.013.9.

McCabe Maryann and Timothy de Waal Malefyt 2013. Creativity and Cooking: Motherhood, Agency and Social Change in Everyday Life. *Journal of Consumer Culture*, 15(1): 48–65.

McCabe, Maryann, Timothy Malefyt, and A. Fabri 2017. Women, Makeup and Authenticity: Negotiating Embodiment and Discourses of Beauty. *Journal of Consumer Culture*, http://dx.doi.org/10.1177/1469540517736558

McCracken, Grant 1988. *The Long Interview*. Thousand Oaks, CA: Sage.

McCracken, Grant 2005. *Culture and Consumption II: Markets, Meaning, and Brand Management*. Bloomington, IN: Indiana University Press.

McCracken, Grant 2022. *Return of the Artisan: How America Went from Industrial to Handmade*. New York: S&S/Simon Element.

Mead, Margaret 1928. *Coming of Age in Samoa*. New York: Morrow.

Mead, Margaret 1930. *Growing Up in New Guinea: A Comparative Study of Primitive Education*. New York: Morrow.

Meyer, D. E., E. Lo, S. Afshari, A. Vaughan, D. Rissolo, and F. Kuester 2016. Utility of Low-cost Drones to Generate 3D Models of Archaeological Sites from Multisensor Data. *The SAA Archaeological Record*, 16(2): 22–24.

Miles, Richard B. (ed.) 2000. *Teaching Music Through Performance in Band*, Volume 3. Chicago, IL: GIA Publications.

Miller Daniel and Heather Horst (eds) 2012. *Digital Anthropology*. London: Bloomsbury.

Miner, Horace 1956. Body Rituals among the Nacirema. *American Anthropologist*, 58(3): 503–507.

Mishan , Ligaya 2020. What is a Tribe? *New York Times*, April 13.

Mitchell, Jon 2014. Anthropologists Behaving Badly? Impact and the Politics of Evaluation in an Era of Accountability. *Etnográfica*, 18(2): 275–297.

Moeran, Brian 2012. Coda in Opinions: What business anthropology is, what it might become… and what, perhaps, it should not be. *Journal of Business Analytics*, 1(2): 290–296.

Moeran, Brian 2014. Theorizing Business and Anthropology in Rita Denny and Patricia Sunderland (eds), *Handbook of Anthropology in Business*. Walnut Creek, CA: Left Coast Press, 69–82.

Moeran, Brian and Timothy de Waal Malefyt 2018. *Magical Capitalism: Enchantment, Spells, and Occult Practices in Contemporary Economics*. New York: Springer.

Morais , Robert 2020. Inspiring Brand Positionings with Mixed Qualitative Methods: A Case of Pet Food. *Journal of Business Analytics*, 9(2): 251–274.

Morais, Robert J. and Timothy de Waal Malefyt 2010. How Anthropologists Can Succeed in Business: Mediating Multiple Worlds of Inquiry. *International Journal of Business Anthropology*, 1(1): 45–56.

Morgan, Blake 2021. 20 Companies that Use Their Profits for Social Good. *Forbes*, available at: https://www.forbes.com/sites/blakemorgan/2021/10/26/20-companies-that-use-their-profits-for-social-good/?sh=7a235d3211a8.

Moussa, Mario, Derek Newberry and Greg Urban 2021. *The Culture Puzzle*. Oakland, CA: Berrett-Koehler.

Muniz, Albert M. and Thomas O'Guinn 2001. Brand Community. *Journal of Consumer Research*, 27: 412–432.

Munk, A. K., Olesen, A. G. and Jacomy, M. 2022. The Thick Machine: Anthropological AI between Explanation and Explication. *Big Data & Society*, 9(1).

Munk , Anders 2023. Coming of Age in Stable Diffusion. *Anthropology News*, 64(2): 29–34.

Munk, Anders Kristian 2019. Four Styles of Quali-quantitative Analysis: Making Sense of the New Nordic Food Movement on the Web. *Nordicom Review*, 40(s1): 159–176.

Munk, Anders Kristian and Anne-Kirstine Bøcher Ellern 2015. Mapping the New Nordic Issue-scape: How to Navigate a Diffuse Controversy with Digital Methods, in Gunnar Thór Johannesson, Carina Ren and René van der Duim (eds), *Tourism Encounters and Controversies: Ontological Politics of Tourism Development*. London: Routledge, 73–96.

Murphy, Keith and George Marcus 2013. Epilogue: Ethnography and Design, Ethnography in Design, Ethnography by Design, in Wendy Gunn, Ton Otto, and Rachel Charlotte Smith (eds), *Design Anthropology: Theory and Practice*, London: Routledge, 251–268.

Murphy, Patrick E., John F. Sherry Jr. 2014. *Marketing and the Common Good: Essays from Notre Dame on Societal Impact*. Abingdon: Routledge.

Nader, Laura 1969. Up the Anthropologist: Perspectives Gained From Studying Up, in D. Hymes (ed.), *Reinventing Anthropology*. New York: Random House.

Nardi, Bonnie 2010. *My Life as a Night Elf Priest: An Anthropological Account of World of Warcraft*. Ann Arbor, MI: University of Michigan Press.

Norman, Donald1988. *The Psychology of Everyday Things*. New York: Basic Books.

Otto, Ton and Rachel Charlotte Smith 1987. *The Anthropology of Performance*. New York: PAJ Publications.

Otto, Ton and Rachel Charlotte Smith 2013. Design Anthropology: A Distinct Style of Knowing, in Wendy Gunn, Ton Otto and Rachel Charlotte Smith (eds), *Design Anthropology: Theory and Practice*. London: Bloomsbury, 1–29.

Paff, Stephen 2021. Anthropology by Data Science. *Annals of Anthropological Practice*, 46(1): 7–18.

Pant, Dipak R. 2014. Management Consulting in Times of Austerity: Sustainability & the Business-Place-Community Nexus in Italy, in Rita Denny and Patricia Sunderland (eds), *Handbook of Anthropology in Business*. Walnut Oak, CA: Left Coast Press, 223–233.

Peacock, James 2002. Action Comparison: Efforts towards a Global and Comparative yet Local and Active Anthropology, in Andre Gingrich and Richard G. Fox (eds), *Anthropology, by Comparison*. London: Taylor & Francis, 44–69.

Pink, Sarah 2021. Digital Futures Anthropology, in Haidy Geismar and Hannah Knox (eds), *Digital Anthropology*(2nd edn). London: Routledge, 307–324.

Pink, Sarah 2022. *Emerging Technologies / Life at the Edge of the Future*. London: Routledge.

Pink, Sarah, Elisenda Ardèvol and Débora Lanzeni (eds) 2016. *Digital Materialities Design and Anthropology*. London: Routledge.

Pink, Sarah, Vaike Fors and Tom O'Dell (eds) 2017. *Theoretical Scholarship and Applied Practice*. New York: Berghahn Books.

Pink, Sarah, Vaike Fors, DeboraLanzeni, MelisaDuque, ShantiSumartojo and Yolande Strengers 2022. *Design Ethnography: Research, Responsibilities, and Futures*. London: Routledge.

Proctor, Devin and Tariq Adely 2021. Care by Emoji. Anthropology News website, available at: https://www.anthropology-news.org/articles/care-by-emoji/.

Powell, Elizabeth 2019. Why Businesses and Consumers Need Us. *Journal of Business Analytics* 8(1): 126–138.

Qustodio 2022. Annual Report: Raising the Digital Generations. Available at: https://www.qustodio.com/en/from-alpha-to-z-raising-the-digital-genera tions/social-media-qustodio-annual-data-report-2022/.

Reese, William 2002. Behavioral Scientists Enter Design: Seven Critical Histories, in Susan Squires and Bryan Byrne (eds), *Creating Breakthrough Ideas: The Collaboration of Anthropologists and Designers in the Product Development Industry*. Westport, CT: Praeger: 17–43.

Redding, Terry and Charles Cheney (eds) 2022. *Profiles of Anthropological Praxis*. New York: Berghahn Books.

Reynolds, Thomas and Jonathan Cutman 1988. Laddering Theory, Method, Analysis, and Interpretation. *Journal of Advertising Research*, February/March.

Rose, Dan 1989. *Patterns of American Culture*. Philadephia, PA: University of Pennsylvania Press.

Sabloff, Jeremy A. 2011. Where Have You Gone, Margaret Mead? *Anthropology and Public Intellectuals*, Augusthttps://doi.org/10.1111/j.1548-1433.2011.01350.x.

Sahlins, Marshall 2013. The National Academy of Sciences: Goodbye to All That. *Anthropology Today*, 29(2): 1–2.

Said, Edward 1973. US Policy and the Conflict of Powers in the Middle East. *Journal of Palestine Studies*, 2(3): 30–50.

Said, Edward 1978. *Orientalism: Western Concepts of the Orient*. New York: Pantheon.

Schwartzman, Helen 1993. *Ethnography in Organizations*. Thousand Oaks, CA: Sage.

Seaver , Nick 2015. Bastard Algebra, in T. Boellstorff and B. Maurer (eds), *Data, Now Bigger and Better*. Chicago, IL: Prickly Paradigm Press, 27–45.

Seaver , Nick 2018. What Should an Anthropology of Algorithms Do? *Cultural Anthropology*, 33(3): 375–385.

Sennett, Richard 2008. *The Craftsman*. New Haven, CT: Yale University Press.

Shaw, Ian G. R. 2016. The Urbanization of Drone Warfare: Policing Surplus Populations in the Dronepolis. *Geographica Helvetica*, 71(1): 19–28.

Sherry, John F. Jr. 2017. Such Bitter Business: Reconciling Ethical Domains in Practice, in Timothy Malefyt and Morais (eds), *Ethics in the Anthropology of Business*. London: Routledge, 44–53.

Sieck, Kate and Laura A. McNamara 2016. *Organizational Culture and Change*. Available at: https://www.epicpeople.org/organizational-culture-and-change/.

Spradley , James P. 1979. *The Ethnographic Interview*. Long Grove, IL: Waveland.

Squires, Susan 2002. Doing the Work: Customer Research in the Product Development and Design Industry, in Susan Squires and Bryan Byrne (eds), *Creating Breakthrough Ideas: The Collaboration of Anthropologists and Designers in the Product Development Industry*, Westport, CT: Praeger, 103–123.

Stronza, Amanda 2022. Ecotourism in One Amazon Community: My Role as Anthropologist, Witness, Scribe, and Facilitator, in Terry Redding and Charles Cheney (eds), *Profiles of Anthropological Praxis*. New York: Berghahn Books, 21–37.

Stoller, P. (2007), Ethnography/Memoir/Imagination/Story. *Anthropology and Humanism*, 32: 178–191. HYPERLINK "https://protect-us.mimecast.com/s/hYUsCwpEkBH0rxKOVhVdnD2?domain=doi.org" https://doi.org/10.1525/ahu.2007.32.2.178

Suchman, Lucy 2011. Anthropological Relocations and the Limits of Design, *Annual Review of Anthropology*, 40:1–18.

Sunderland, Patricia L. and Denny, Rita M. 2003. Psychology vs. Anthropology: Where is Culture in Marketplace Ethnography? in T. Malefyt and B. Moeran (eds), *Advertising Cultures*. Oxford: Berg, 187–202.

Sunderland, Patricia and Rita Denny 2007. *Doing Anthropology in Consumer Research*. Walnut Creek, CA: Left Coast Press.

Tett, Gillian 2015. *Silo Effect. The Peril of Expertise and the Promise of Breaking Down Barriers*. Simon and Schuster.

Tett, Gillian 2021. *Anthro-Vision: A New Way to See in Business and Life*. London: Penguin.

The Economist 2012. Crunching the Numbers. 19 May. Available at: https://www.economist.com/special-report/2012/05/19/crunching-the-numbers#.

Thrift, Nigel 2005. *Knowing Capitalism*. London: Sage.

Tsing, Anna 2010. Worlding the Matsutake Diaspora: Or, Can Actor-Network Theory Experiment with Holism? in Ton Otto and Nils Bubandt (eds), *Experiments in Holism*. Oxford: Wiley-Blackwell, 47–66.

Turner, Victor 1969. *The Ritual Process: Structure and Anti-Structure*. New York: Aldine.

Turner, Victor W. 1987. *The Anthropology of Performance*. New York: PAJ Publications.

Underhill, Paco 2008. *Why We Buy*. New York: Simon and Schuster.

Urban, Greg 2001. *Metaculture: How Culture Moves through the World*. Minneapolis, MN: University of Minnesota Press.

Vanhemert, Kyle 2014. Why *Her* Will Dominate UI Design Even More Than *Minority Report*. Available at: http://www.wired.com/2014/01/will-influential-ui-design-minority-report/ [Accessed 11 August 2014].

Von Hippel, Eric 2005. *Democratizing Innovation*. Cambridge, MA: MIT Press.

Wakefield, Jane 2013. Tomorrow's Cities: How Big Data Is Changing the World. BBC News, 27 August. Available at: https://www.bbc.co.uk/news/technology-23253949.

Wang, Tricia May 2013. Big Data Needs Thick Data. *Ethnography Matters*. Available at: http://ethnographymatters.net/2013/05/13/big-data-needs-thick-data/.

Wang, Tricia 2014. Live Fieldnoting: Creating More Open Ethnography, in Rita Denny and Patricia Sunderland (eds), *Handbook of Anthropology in Business*. London: Routledge, 638–657.

Wasson, Christina 2000. Ethnography in the Field of Design. *Human Organization*, 59(4): 377–388.

While, Aidan H., Simon Marvin and Mateja Kovacic 2021. Urban Robotic Experimentation: San Francisco, Tokyo and Dubai. *Urban Studies*, 58(4): 769–786.

Willis, Mark, Chester Walker and Eleanor Harrison-Buck 2016. Using Drones in a Threatened Archaeological Landscape: Rapid Survey, Salvage, and Mapping of the Maya Site of Saturday Creek, Belize. *The Society for American Archaeology. The SAA Archaeological Record*, 16(2): 30–35.

INDEX

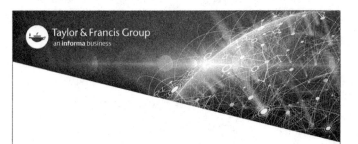

Printed in the United States
by Baker & Taylor Publisher Services